THE POOH
BOOK OF
QUOTATIONS

D1392669

A.A.Milne

The Pooh Book of Quotations

In which will be found some
Useful Information and Sustaining Thoughts
by Winnie-the-Pooh and his friends

Compiled by Brian Sibley

With illustrations by E.H.Shepard

MAMMOTH

Also available in Mammoth

Winnie-the-Pooh
The House at Pooh Corner
Now We Are Six
When We Were Very Young

Pooh & Piglet *picture books, each a memorable chapter from*
Winnie-the-Pooh *or* The House at Pooh Corner.

First published in Great Britain 1986
by Methuen Children's Books
This edition first published 1993 by Mammoth
an imprint of Reed Consumer Books Limited
Michelin House, 81 Fulham Road, London SW3 6RB
and Auckland, Melbourne, Singapore and Toronto

Reprinted 1994

Copyright © 1986 by Michael John Brown, Peter Janson-Smith,
Roger Hugh Vaughan Charles Morgan and Timothy Michael Robinson,
Trustees of the Pooh Properties.
Text by A.A. Milne and line Illustrations by E.H. Shepard
from *Winnie-the-Pooh, The House at Pooh Corner,
When We Were Very Young* and *Now We Are Six,*
Copyright under the Berne Convention.
Introduction and compilation copyright © 1986 by Brian Sibley.

ISBN 0 7497 1261 9

A CIP record for this title is available
from the British Library

Printed and bound in Great Britain
by Cox & Wyman Ltd, Reading, Berkshire

This paperback is sold subject to the condition
that it shall not, by way of trade or otherwise,
be lent, resold, hired out, or otherwise circulated
without the publisher's prior consent in any form
of binding or cover other than that in which
it is published and without a similar condition
including this condition being imposed
on the subsequent purchaser.

CONTENTS

INTRODUCTION

Despite being a self-confessed Bear of Very Little Brain, Winnie-the-Pooh has managed some startling Thoughts and said some extraordinary Things. So much so, that his Publisher decided that it would be a Good Plan to collect them together into a Useful Book.

The trouble is, all the Others got to hear about it and started complaining that they were being Left Out, and that it couldn't possibly be a Useful Book unless some of their Remarks and Observations were put in as well. So that is what we did – although it is still called *The Pooh Book of Quotations*.

While we were about it, we also included – in addition to extracts from *Winnie-the-Pooh* and *The House at Pooh Corner* – one or two quotations from *When We Were Very Young* and *Now We Are Six*, either because they were about Christopher Robin or Pooh or Both, or just because we liked them.

The quotations have been gathered together according to their subject, such as 'Food' and 'Weather' (two of the most popular topics of conversation in the 100 Aker Wood). And, at the end of the book, you will find an Index, where you can look up specific things like 'Condensed Milk' and 'Earthquakes', and find out Who said What, When, about Which, and Why; and that makes it a Very Useful Book Indeed.

Brian Sibley

SHORT FOR
TRESPASSERS
WILLIAM

In which we find Quotations about Names

Once upon a time, a very long time ago now, about last Friday, Winnie-the-Pooh lived in a forest all by himself under the name of Sanders.

(*"What does 'under the name' mean?" asked Christopher Robin.*

"It means he had the name over the door in gold letters and lived under it.")

Winnie-the-Pooh

Edward Bear, known to his friends as Winnie-the-Pooh, or Pooh for short, was walking through the Forest one day, humming proudly to himself.

Winnie-the-Pooh

When I first heard his name, I said, just as you are going to say, "But I thought he was a boy?"

"So did I," said Christopher Robin.

"Then you can't call him Winnie?"

"I don't."

"But you said—"

"He's Winnie-ther-Pooh. Don't you know what '*ther*' means?"

"Ah, yes, now I do," I said quickly; and I hope you do too, because it is all the explanation you are going to get.

Winnie-the-Pooh

Christopher Robin, who feeds this swan in the mornings, has given him the name of "Pooh". This is a very fine name for a swan, because, if you call him and he doesn't come (which is a thing swans are good at), then you can pretend that you were just saying "Pooh!" to show how little you wanted him.

When We Were Very Young

If you happen to have read another book about Christopher Robin, you may remember that he once had a swan (or the swan had Christopher Robin, I don't know which), and that he used to call this swan Pooh. That was a long time ago, and when we said good-bye, we took the name with us, as we didn't think the swan would want it any more. Well, when Edward Bear said that he would like an exciting name all to himself, Christopher Robin said at once, without stopping to think, that he was Winnie-the-Pooh. And he was. So, as I have explained the Pooh part, I will now explain the rest of it.

... when Christopher Robin goes to the Zoo, he goes to where the Polar Bears are, and he whispers something to the third keeper from the left, and doors are unlocked, and we wander through dark passages and up steep stairs, until at last we come to the special cage, and the cage is opened, and out trots something brown and furry, and with a happy cry of "Oh, Bear!" Christopher Robin rushes into its arms. Now this bear's name is Winnie, which shows what a good name for bears it is, but the funny thing is that we can't remember whether Winnie is called after Pooh, or Pooh after Winnie. We did know once, but we have forgotten ...

Winnie-the-Pooh

What shall I call
  My dear little dormouse?
His eyes are small,
  But his tail is e-nor-mouse

I sometimes call him Terrible John,
'Cos his tail goes on –
And on –
And on.
And I sometimes call him Terrible Jack,
'Cos his tail goes on to the end of his back.
And I sometimes call him Terrible James,
'Cos he says he likes me calling him names. ...

But I think I shall call him Jim,
'Cos I *am* fond of him.

When We Were Very Young

Next to his house was a piece of broken board which had: "TRESPASSERS W" on it. When Christopher Robin asked the Piglet what it meant, he said it was his grandfather's name, and had been in the family for a long time. Christopher Robin said you *couldn't* be called Trespassers W, and Piglet said yes, you could, because his grandfather was, and it was short for Trespassers Will, which was short for Trespassers William. And his grandfather had had two names in case he lost one – Trespassers after an uncle, and William after Trespassers.

"I've got two names," said Christopher Robin carelessly.

"Well, there you are, that proves it," said Piglet.

Winnie-the-Pooh

11

But his arms were so stiff from holding on to the string of the balloon all that time that they stayed up straight in the air for more than a week, and whenever a fly came and settled on his nose he had to blow it off. And I think – but I am not sure – that *that* is why he was always called Pooh.

Winnie-the-Pooh

"I knew it wasn't Piglet," said Kanga. "I wonder who it can be."

"Perhaps it's some relation of Pooh's," said Christopher Robin. "What about a nephew or an uncle or something?"

Kanga agreed that this was probably what it was, and said that they would have to call it by some name.

"I shall call it Pootel," said Christopher Robin. "Henry Pootel for short."

Winnie-the-Pooh

I found a little beetle, so that Beetle
 was his name,
And I called him Alexander and he
 answered just the same.
I put him in a match-box, and I
 kept him all the day . . .
And Nanny let my beetle out –

Yes, Nanny let my beetle out –

Small's real name was Very Small Beetle, but he was called Small for short, when he was spoken to at all, which hardly ever happened except when somebody said: "*Really*, Small!" He had been staying with Christopher Robin for a few seconds, and he had started round a gorse-bush for exercise, but instead of coming back the other way, as expected, he hadn't, so nobody knew where he was.

The House at Pooh Corner

She went and let my beetle
 out –

And Beetle ran away.

Now We Are Six

NO BRAIN
AT ALL

In which we find Quotations about Having Brains and Having Grey Fluff

"Pooh," said Rabbit kindly, "you haven't any brain."

"I know," said Pooh humbly.

Winnie-the-Pooh

Pooh sat down on a large stone, and tried to think this out. It sounded to him like a riddle, and he was never much good at riddles, being a Bear of Very Little Brain.

Winnie-the-Pooh

Pooh knew what he meant, but, being a Bear of Very Little Brain, couldn't think of the words.

The House at Pooh Corner

"Rabbit's clever," said Pooh thoughtfully.

"Yes," said Piglet, "Rabbit's clever."

"And he has Brain."

"Yes," said Piglet, "Rabbit has Brain."

There was a long silence.

"I suppose," said Pooh, "that that's why he never understands anything."

The House at Pooh Corner

"Do you think they're all right, Owl?"

"I expect so. You see, at any moment—"

"Do go and see, Owl. Because Pooh hasn't got very much brain, and he might do something silly, and I do love him so, Owl. Do you see, Owl?"

"That's all right," said Owl. "I'll go. Back directly."

And he flew off.

Winnie-the-Pooh

13

"And if anyone knows anything about anything," said Bear to himself, "it's Owl who knows something about something," he said, "or my name's not Winnie-the-Pooh," he said. "Which it is," he added. "So there you are."

Winnie-the-Pooh

"And I said to myself: The others will be sorry if I'm getting myself all cold. They haven't got Brains, any of them, only grey fluff that's blown into their heads by mistake, and they don't Think, but if it goes on snowing for another six weeks or so, one of them will begin to say to himself: 'Eeyore can't be so very much too Hot about three o'clock in the morning.' And then it will Get About. And they'll be Sorry."

The House at Pooh Corner

"There's Pooh," he thought to himself. "Pooh hasn't much Brain, but he never comes to any harm. He does silly things and they turn out right. There's Owl. Owl hasn't exactly got Brain, but he Knows Things. He would know the Right Thing to Do when Surrounded by Water. There's Rabbit. He hasn't Learnt in Books, but he can always Think of a Clever Plan. There's Kanga. She isn't Clever, Kanga isn't, but she would be so anxious about Roo that she would do a Good Thing to Do without thinking about it. And then there's Eeyore. And Eeyore is so miserable anyhow that he wouldn't mind about this. But I wonder what Christopher Robin would do?"

Winnie-the-Pooh

"Yes," said Winnie-the-Pooh.

"I see now," said Winnie-the-Pooh.

"I have been Foolish and Deluded," said he, "and I am a Bear of No Brain at All."

"You're the Best Bear in All the World," said Christopher Robin soothingly.

"Am I?" said Pooh hopefully. And then he brightened up suddenly.

"Anyhow," he said, "it is nearly Luncheon Time."

So he went home for it.

Winnie-the-Pooh

Pooh was saying to himself, "If only I could *think* of something!" For he felt sure that a Very Clever Brain could catch a Heffalump if only he knew the right way to go about it.

Winnie-the-Pooh

"After all," said Rabbit to himself, "Christopher Robin depends on Me. He's fond of Pooh and Piglet and Eeyore, and so am I, but they haven't any Brain. Not to notice. And he respects Owl, because you can't help respecting anybody who can spell TUESDAY, even if he doesn't spell it right; but spelling isn't everything. There are days when spelling Tuesday simply doesn't count. And Kanga is too busy looking after Roo, and Roo is too young and Tigger is too bouncy to be of any help, so there's really nobody but Me, when you come to look at it. I'll go and see if there's anything he wants doing, and then I'll do it for him. It's just the day for doing things."

The House at Pooh Corner

"You're sure it *was* a house?" said Pooh. "I mean, you're sure the house was just here?"

"Of course I am," said Eeyore. And he murmured to himself, "No brain at all, some of them."

The House at Pooh Corner

Well, Pooh was a Bear of Enormous
  Brain –
(*Just say it again!*)
Of enormous brain –
(*Of enormous what?*)
Well, he ate a lot.

Winnie-the-Pooh

"It just shows what can be done by taking a little trouble," said Eeyore. "Do you see, Pooh? Do you see, Piglet? Brains first and then Hard Work. Look at it! *That's* the way to build a house," said Eeyore proudly.

The House at Pooh Corner

15

AN OLD WORLD RESIDENCE OF GREAT CHARM

In which we find Quotations about Houses and Homes

"I've been thinking," said Pooh, "and what I've been thinking is this. I've been thinking about Eeyore."

"What about Eeyore?"

"Well, poor Eeyore has nowhere to live."

"Nor he has," said Piglet.

"*You* have a house, Piglet, and I have a house, and they are very good houses. And Christopher Robin has a house, and Owl and Kanga and Rabbit have houses, and even Rabbit's friends and relations have houses or somethings, but poor Eeyore has nothing. So what I've been thinking is: Let's build him a house."

"That," said Piglet, "is a Grand Idea. Where shall we build it?"

"We will build it here," said Pooh, "just by this wood, out of the wind, because this is where I thought of it. And we will call this Pooh Corner. And we will build an Eeyore House with sticks at Pooh Corner for Eeyore."

The House at Pooh Corner

Now Teddy, as was only right,
Slept in the ottoman at night,
And with him crowded in as well
More animals than I can tell;
Not only these, but books and things,
Such as a kind relation brings –
Old tales of "Once upon a time,"
And history retold in rhyme.

When We Were Very Young

"There was a heap of sticks on the other side of the wood," said Piglet. "I saw them. Lots and lots. All piled up."

"Thank you, Piglet," said Pooh. "What you have just said will be a Great Help to us, and because of it I could call this place Poohanpiglet Corner if Pooh Corner didn't sound better, which it does, being smaller and more like a corner. Come along."

The House at Pooh Corner

Owl lived at The Chestnuts, an old-world residence of great charm, which was grander than anybody else's, or seemed so to Bear, because it had both a knocker *and* a bell-pull.

Winnie-the-Pooh

17

I have a house where I go
   When there's too many people,
I have a house where I go
   Where no one can be;
I have a house where I go,
Where nobody ever says "No"
Where no one says anything – so
   There is no one but me.

Now We Are Six

The Piglet lived in a very grand house in the middle of a beech-tree, and the beech-tree was in the middle of the Forest, and the Piglet lived in the middle of the house.

Winnie-the-Pooh

"What's the matter, Eeyore?"

"Nothing, Christopher Robin. Nothing important. I suppose you haven't seen a house or what-not anywhere about?"

"What sort of a house?"

"Just a house."

"Who lives there?"

"I do. At least I thought I did. But I suppose I don't. After all, we can't all have houses."

The House at Pooh Corner

So what it all comes to is that I built myself a house down by my little wood."

"Did you really? How exciting!"

"The really exciting part," said Eeyore in his most melancholy voice, "is that when I left it this morning it was there, and when I came back it wasn't. Not at all, very natural, and it was only Eeyore's house. But still I just wondered."

The House at Pooh Corner

"We can't get down, we can't get down!" cried Roo. "Isn't it fun? Pooh, isn't it fun, Tigger and I are living in a tree, like Owl, and we're going to stay here for ever and ever. I can see Piglet's house. Piglet, I can see your house from here. Aren't we high? Is Owl's house as high up as this?"

The House at Pooh Corner

18

"If only," he thought, as he looked out of the window, "I had been in Pooh's house, or Christopher Robin's house, or Rabbit's house when it began to rain, then I should have had Company all this time, instead of being here all alone, with nothing to do except wonder when it will stop." And he imagined himself with Pooh, saying, "Did you ever see such rain, Pooh?" and Pooh saying, "Isn't it *awful*, Piglet?" and Piglet saying, "I wonder how it is over Christopher Robin's way," and Pooh saying, "I should think poor old Rabbit is about flooded out by this time." It would have been jolly to talk like this, and really, it wasn't much good having anything exciting like floods, if you couldn't share them with somebody.

Winnie-the-Pooh

I went into a house, and it wasn't a house,
　It has big steps and a great
　big hall;
But it hasn't got a garden,
　　A garden,
　　A garden,
　It isn't like a house at all.

When We Were Very Young

"Sometimes," said Eeyore, "when people have quite finished taking a person's house, there are one or two bits which they don't want and are rather glad for the person to take back, if you know what I mean.

The House at Pooh Corner

Now one autumn morning when the wind had blown all the leaves off the trees in the night, and was trying to blow the branches off, Pooh and Piglet were sitting in the Thoughtful Spot and wondering.

"What *I* think," said Pooh, "is I think we'll go to Pooh Corner and see Eeyore, because perhaps his house has been blown down, and perhaps he'd like us to build it again."

The House at Pooh Corner

19

Pooh had wandered into the Hundred Acre Wood, and was standing in front of what had once been Owl's House. It didn't look at all like a house now; it looked like a tree which had been blown down; and as soon as a house looks like that, it is time you tried to find another one.

The House at Pooh Corner

"It's like this," said Piglet quickly.... "Only warmer," he added after deep thought.

"What's warmer?"

"The other side of the wood, where Eeyore's house is."

"*My* house?" said Eeyore. "My house was here."

"No," said Piglet firmly. "The other side of the wood."

"Because of being warmer," said Pooh.

"But I ought to *know*—"

"Come and look," said Piglet simply, and he led the way.

"There wouldn't be *two* houses," said Pooh. "Not so close together."

They came round the corner, and there was Eeyore's house, looking as comfy as anything.

"There you are," said Piglet.

"Inside as well as outside," said Pooh proudly.

The House at Pooh Corner

"It's a remarkable thing," he said. "It *is* my house, and I built it where I said I did, so the wind must have blown it here. And the wind blew it right over the wood, and blew it down here, and here it is as good as ever. In fact, better in places."

The House at Pooh Corner

"I have been told – the news has worked through to my corner of the Forest – the damp bit down on the right which nobody wants – that a certain Person is looking for a house. I have found one for him."

The House at Pooh Corner

"Hallo, Eeyore," they called out cheerfully.

"Ah!" said Eeyore. "Lost your way?"

"We just came to see you," said Piglet. "And to see how your house was. Look, Pooh, it's still standing!"

"I know," said Eeyore. "Very odd. Somebody ought to have come down and pushed it over."

"We wondered whether the wind would blow it down," said Pooh.

"Ah, that's why nobody's bothered, I suppose. I thought perhaps they'd forgotten."

The House at Pooh Corner

"There!" said Eeyore proudly, stopping them outside Piglet's house. "And the name on it, and everything!"

"Oh!" cried Christopher Robin, wondering whether to laugh or what.

"Just the house for Owl. Don't you think so, little Piglet?"

And then Piglet did a Noble Thing, and he did it in a sort of dream, while he was thinking of all the wonderful words Pooh had hummed about him.

"Yes, it's just the house for Owl," he said grandly. "And I hope he'll be very happy in it." And then he gulped twice, because he had been very happy in it himself.

The House at Pooh Corner

"Well," he said at last, "it's a very nice house, and if your own house is blown down, you *must* go somewhere else, mustn't you, Piglet? What would *you* do, if *your* house was blown down?"

Before Piglet could think, Pooh answered for him.

"He'd come and live with me," said Pooh, "wouldn't you, Piglet?"

Piglet squeezed his paw.

"Thank you, Pooh," he said, "I should love to."

The House at Pooh Corner

21

A LITTLE SMACKEREL
OF SOMETHING

*In which we find Quotations
about Things to Eat
and Eating Too Much*

He looked up at his clock, which had stopped at five minutes to eleven some weeks ago.

"Nearly eleven o'clock," said Pooh happily. "You're just in time for a little smackerel of something," and he put his head into the cupboard.

The House at Pooh Corner

"Well," said Pooh, "it's the middle of the night, which is a good time for going to sleep. And to-morrow morning we'll have some honey for breakfast. Do Tiggers like honey?"

"They like everything," said Tigger cheerfully.

The House at Pooh Corner

Binker isn't greedy, but he does
  like things to eat,
So I have to say to people when
  they're giving me a sweet,
"Oh, Binker wants a chocolate, so
  could you give me two?"
And then I eat it for him, 'cos his
  teeth are rather new.

Now We Are Six

A bear, however hard he tries,
Grows tubby without exercise.
Our Teddy Bear is short and fat,
Which is not to be wondered at;
He gets what exercise he can
By falling off the ottoman,
But generally seems to lack
The energy to clamber back.

When We Were Very Young

And it was eleven o'clock.
Which was Time-for-a-little-
    something. . . .

The House at Pooh Corner

As soon as he got home, he went to the larder; and he stood on a chair, and took down a very large jar of honey from the top shelf. It had HUNNY written on it, but, just to make sure, he took off the paper cover and looked at it, and it *looked* just like honey. "But you never can tell," said Pooh. "I remember my uncle saying once that he had seen cheese just this colour." So he put his tongue in, and took a large lick. "Yes," he said, "it is. No doubt about that. And honey, I should say, right down to the bottom of the jar. Unless, of course," he said, "somebody put cheese in at the bottom just for a joke. Perhaps I had better go a *little* further . . . just in case . . . in case Heffalumps *don't* like cheese . . . same as me . . . Ah!" And he gave a deep sigh. "I *was* right. It *is* honey, right the way down."

Winnie-the-Pooh

One day when he was out walking, he came to an open place in the middle of the forest, and in the middle of this place was a large oak-tree, and, from the top of the tree, there came a loud buzzing noise.

Winnie-the-Pooh sat down at the foot of the tree, put his head between his paws, and began to think.

First of all he said to himself: "That buzzing-noise means something. You don't get a buzzing-noise like that, just buzzing and buzzing, without its meaning something. If there's a buzzing-noise, somebody's making a buzzing-noise, and the only reason for making a buzzing-noise that *I* know of is because you're a bee."

Then he thought another long time, and said: "And the only reason for being a bee that I know of is making honey."

And then he got up, and said: "And the only reason for making honey is so as *I* can eat it."

Winnie-the-Pooh

"Rabbit," said Pooh to himself. "I *like* talking to Rabbit. He talks about sensible things. He doesn't use long, difficult words, like Owl. He uses short, easy words, like 'What about lunch?' and 'Help yourself, Pooh.' I suppose, *really*, I ought to go and see Rabbit."

The House at Pooh Corner

And we must all bring Provisions."

"Bring what?"

"Things to eat."

"Oh!" said Pooh happily. "I thought you said Provisions. I'll go and tell them." And he stumped off.

Winnie-the-Pooh

And as soon as they sat down, Tigger took a large mouthful of honey ... and he looked up at the ceiling with his head on one side, and made exploring noises with his tongue, and considering noises, and what-have-we-got-*here* noises ... and then he said in a very decided voice:

"Tiggers don't like honey"

"Oh!" said Pooh, and tried to make it sound Sad and Regretful. "I thought they liked everything."

"Everything except honey," said Tigger.

The House at Pooh Corner

What is the matter with Mary Jane?
She's perfectly well and she hasn't a pain,
And it's lovely rice pudding for dinner again!—
What *is* the matter with Mary Jane?

When We Were Very Young

"I think," said Christopher Robin, "that we ought to eat all our Provisions now, so that we shan't have so much to carry."

"Eat all our what?" said Pooh.

"All that we've brought," said Piglet, getting to work.

"That's a good idea," said Pooh, and he got to work too.

Winnie-the-Pooh

"A Reward!" said Owl very loudly. "We write a notice to say that we will give a large something to anybody who finds Eeyore's tail."

"I see, I see," said Pooh, nodding his head. "Talking about large somethings," he went on dreamily, "I generally have a small something about now – about this time in the morning," and he looked wistfully at the cupboard in the corner of Owl's parlour; "just a mouthful of condensed milk or what-not, with perhaps a lick of honey—"

Winnie-the-Pooh

Pooh always liked a little something at eleven o'clock in the morning, and he was very glad to see Rabbit getting out the plates and mugs; and when Rabbit said, "Honey or condensed milk with your bread?" he was so excited that he said, "Both," and then, so as not to seem greedy, he added, "But don't bother about the bread, please." And for a long time after that he said nothing ... until at last, humming to himself in a rather sticky voice, he got up, shook Rabbit lovingly by the paw, and said that he must be going on.

"Well, good-bye, if you're sure you won't have any more."

"*Is* there any more?" asked Pooh quickly.

Rabbit took the covers off the dishes, and said, "No, there wasn't."

"I thought not," said Pooh, nodding to himself.

Winnie-the-Pooh

"It all comes," said Pooh crossly, "of not having front doors big enough."

"It all comes," said Rabbit sternly, "of eating too much. I thought at the time," said Rabbit, "only I didn't like to say anything," said Rabbit, "that one of us was eating too much," said Rabbit, "and I knew it wasn't *me*,' he said.

Winnie-the-Pooh

"Tiggers don't like haycorns."

"But you said they liked everything except honey," said Pooh.

"Everything except honey *and* haycorns," explained Tigger.

The House at Pooh Corner

Isn't it funny
How a bear likes honey?
Buzz! Buzz! Buzz!
I wonder why he does?

Winnie-the-Pooh

Pooh's friend stopped shaking his head to get the prickles out, and explained that Tiggers didn't like thistles.

"Then why bend a perfectly good one?" asked Eeyore.

"But you said," began Pooh, "— you *said* that Tiggers liked everything except honey and haycorns."

"*And* thistles," said Tigger, who was now running round in circles with his tongue hanging out.

The House at Pooh Corner

"Now then, Piglet, let's go home."

"But, Pooh," cried Piglet, all excited, "do you know the way?"

"No," said Pooh. "But there are twelve pots of honey in my cupboard, and they've been calling to me for hours. I couldn't hear them properly before because Rabbit *would* talk, but if nobody says anything except those twelve pots, I *think*, Piglet, I shall know where they're coming from. Come on."

The House at Pooh Corner

He splashed to his door and looked out. . . .

"This is Serious," said Pooh. "I must have an Escape."

So he took his largest pot of honey and escaped with it to a broad branch of his tree, well above the water, and then he climbed down again and escaped with another pot ... and when the whole Escape was finished, there was Pooh sitting on his branch, dangling his legs, and there, beside him, were ten pots of honey. . . .

Two days later, there was Pooh, sitting on his branch, dangling his legs, and there, beside him, were four pots of honey. . . .

Three days later, there was Pooh, sitting on his branch, dangling his legs, and there beside him, was one pot of honey.

Four days later, there was Pooh . . .

Winnie-the-Pooh

Pooh was sitting in his house one day, counting his pots of honey, when there came a knock on the door.

"Fourteen," said Pooh. "Come in. Fourteen. Or was it fifteen? Bother. That's muddled me."

"Hallo, Pooh," said Rabbit.

"Fourteen, that's right."

"Are you sure?"

"No," said Rabbit. "Does it matter?"

"I just like to know," said Pooh humbly. "So as I can say to myself: 'I've got fourteen pots of honey left.' Or fifteen, as the case may be. It's sort of comforting."

"Well, let's call it sixteen," said Rabbit.

"Hallo, Rabbit. Fourteen, wasn't it?"

"What was?"

"My pots of honey what I was counting."

The House at Pooh Corner

At breakfast that morning (a simple meal of marmalade spread lightly over a honeycomb or two) he had suddenly thought of a new song. It began like this:

"*Sing Ho! for the life of a Bear.*"

Winnie-the-Pooh

"I've been finding things in the Forest," said Tigger importantly. "I've found a pooh and a piglet and an eeyore, but I can't find any breakfast."

The House at Pooh Corner

The King said,
"Bother!"
And then he said,
"Oh, deary me!"
The King sobbed, "Oh, deary me!"
And went back to bed.
"Nobody,"
He whimpered,
"Could call me
A fussy man;
I *only* want
A little bit
Of butter for
My bread!"

When We Were Very Young

Kanga said to Roo, "Drink up your milk first, dear, and talk afterwards." So Roo, who was drinking his milk, tried to say that he could do both at once ... and had to be patted on the back and dried for quite a long time afterwards.

Winnie-the-Pooh

Roo was silent for a little while, and then he said, "Shall we eat our sandwiches, Tigger?" And Tigger said, "Yes, where are they?" And Roo said, "At the bottom of the tree." And Tigger said, "I don't think we'd better eat them just yet." So they didn't.

The House at Pooh Corner

27

"He's taken my medicine, he's taken my medicine, he's taken my medicine!" sang Roo happily, thinking it was a tremendous joke.

Then Tigger looked up at the ceiling, and closed his eyes, and his tongue went round and round his chops, in case he had left any outside, and a peaceful smile came over his face as he said, "So *that's* what Tiggers like!"

The House at Pooh Corner

"Pooh," he said. "Christopher Robin is giving a party."

"Oh!" said Pooh. And then seeing that Owl expected him to say something else, he said, "Will there be those little cake things with pink sugar icing?"

Owl felt that it was rather beneath him to talk about little cake things with pink sugar icing, so he told Pooh exactly what Christopher Robin had said, and flew off to Eeyore.

Winnie-the-Pooh

"Dear, dear," said Pooh, "I didn't know it was as late as that." So he sat down and took the top off his jar of honey. "Lucky I brought this with me," he thought. "Many a bear going out on a warm day like this would never have thought of bringing a little something with him." And he began to eat.

"Now let me see," he thought, as he took his last lick of the inside of the jar, "where was I going? Ah, yes, Eeyore." He got up slowly.

And then, suddenly, he remembered. He had eaten Eeyore's birthday present!

Winnie-the-Pooh

"It all comes, I suppose," he decided, as he said good-bye to the last branch, spun round three times, and flew gracefully into a gorse-bush, "it all comes of *liking* honey so much. Oh, help!"

Winnie-the-Pooh

"Let's go and see *everybody*," said Pooh. "Because when you've been walking in the wind for miles, and you suddenly go into some-body's house, and he says, 'Hallo, Pooh, you're just in time for a little smackerel of something,' and you are, then it's what I call a Friendly Day."

The House at Pooh Corner

29

When Christopher Robin had nailed it on in its right place again, Eeyore frisked about the forest, waving his tail so happily that Winnie-the-Pooh came over all funny, and had to hurry home for a little snack of something to sustain him.

Winnie-the-Pooh

I'd made up a little basket,

just a little,
fair-sized basket,

an ordinary biggish sort of basket, full of—"

The House at Pooh Corner

"Shall I look, too?" said Pooh, who was beginning to feel a little eleven o'clockish. And he found a small tin of condensed milk, and something seemed to tell him that Tiggers didn't like this, so he took it into a corner by itself, and went with it to see that nobody interrupted it.

The House at Pooh Corner

Some hours later, just as the night was beginning to steal away, Pooh woke up suddenly with a sinking feeling. He had had that sinking feeling before, and he knew what it meant. *He was hungry*. So he went to the larder, and he stood on a chair and reached up to the top shelf, and found – nothing.

"That's funny," he thought. "I know I had a jar of honey there. A full jar, full of honey right up to the top, and it had HUNNY written on it, so that I should know it was honey. That's very funny." And then he began to wander up and down, wondering where it was and murmuring to himself. Like this:

It's very, very funny,
'Cos I *know* I had some honey;
'Cos it had a label on,
   Saying HUNNY

A goloptious full-up pot too,
And I don't know where it's got to,
No, I don't know where it's gone –
   Well, it's funny.

Winnie-the-Pooh

It was a warm day, and he had a long way to go. He hadn't gone more than half-way when a sort of funny feeling began to creep all over him. It began at the tip of his nose and trickled all through him and out at the soles of his feet. It was just as if somebody inside him were saying, "Now then, Pooh, time for a little something."

Winnie-the-Pooh

UNFAVOURABLE ATMOSPHERIC CONDITIONS

In which we find Quotations about the Weather

"I don't know how it is, Christopher Robin, but what with all this snow and one thing and another, not to mention icicles and such-like, it isn't so Hot in my field about three o'clock in the morning as some people think it is. It isn't Close, if you know what I mean – not so as to be uncomfortable. It isn't Stuffy. In fact, Christopher Robin," he went on in a loud whisper, "quite-between-ourselves-and-don't-tell-anybody, it's Cold."

The House at Pooh Corner

"I say, Owl," said Christopher Robin, "isn't this fun? I'm on an island!"

"The atmospheric conditions have been very unfavourable lately," said Owl.

"The what?"

"It has been raining," explained Owl.

"Yes," said Christopher Robin. "It has."

"The floodlevel has reached an unprecedented height."

"The who?"

"There's a lot of water about," explained Owl.

"Yes," said Christopher Robin, "there is."

Winnie-the-Pooh

"Hallo, Eeyore!" said Roo.

Eeyore nodded gloomily at him. "It will rain soon, you see if it doesn't," he said.

Roo looked to see if it didn't. and it didn't.

Winnie-the-Pooh

Every morning he went out with his umbrella and put a stick in the place where the water came up to, and every next morning he went out and couldn't see his stick any more, so he put another stick in the place where the water came up to, and then he walked home again, and each morning he had a shorter way to walk than he had had the morning before. On the morning of the fifth day he saw the water all round him, and knew that for the first time in his life he was on a real island. Which was very exciting.

Winnie-the-Pooh

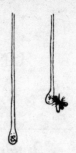

These are my two drops of rain
Waiting on the window-pane

I am waiting here to see
Which the winning one will be.

Both of them have different names.
One is John and one is James.

All the best and all the worst
Comes from which of them is first.

James had just begun to ooze.
He's the one I want to lose.

John is waiting to begin
He's the one I want to win.

James is going slowly on.
Something sort of sticks to John.

John is moving off at last.
James is going pretty fast.

John is rushing down the pane.
James is going slow again.

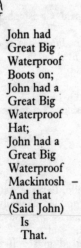

John had
Great Big
Waterproof
Boots on;
John had a
Great Big
Waterproof
Hat;
John had a
Great Big
Waterproof
Mackintosh –
And that
(Said John)
Is
That.

James has met a sort of smear.
John is getting very near.

Is he going fast enough?
(James has found a piece of fluff.)

John has hurried quickly by.
(James was talking to a fly.)

John is there, and John has won!
Look! I told you! Here's the sun!

Now We Are Six

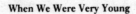

When We Were Very Young

It rained and it rained and it rained. Piglet told himself that never in all his life, and *he* was goodness knows *how* old – three, was it, or four? – never had he seen so much rain. Days and days and days.

Winnie-the-Pooh

"I shouldn't be surprised if it hailed a good deal tomorrow," Eeyore was saying. "Blizzards and what-not. Being fine to-day doesn't Mean Anything. It has no sig – what's that word? Well, it has none of that. It's just a small piece of weather."

The House at Pooh Corner

The next day was quite a different day. Instead of being hot and sunny, it was cold and misty. Pooh didn't mind for himself, but when he thought of all the honey the bees wouldn't be making, a cold and misty day always made him feel sorry for them.

The House at Pooh Corner

One day Rabbit and Piglet were sitting outside Pooh's front door listening to Rabbit, and Pooh was sitting with them. It was a drowsy summer afternoon, and the Forest was full of gentle sounds, which all seemed to be saying to Pooh, "Don't listen to Rabbit, listen to me." So he got into a comfortable position for not listening to Rabbit, and from time to time he opened his eyes to say "Ah!" and then closed them again to say "True," and from time to time Rabbit said, "You see what I mean, Piglet," very earnestly, and Piglet nodded earnestly to show that he did.

The House at Pooh Corner

"Correct me if I am wrong," he said, "but am I right in supposing that it is a very Blusterous day outside?"

"Very," said Piglet, who was quietly thawing his ears, and wishing that he was safely back in his own house.

"I thought so," said Owl. It was on just such a blusterous day as this that my Uncle Robert, a portrait of whom you see upon the wall on your right, Piglet, while returning in the late forenoon from a—What's that?"

There was a loud cracking noise. . . .

The House at Pooh Corner

"Good-bye," said Eeyore. "Mind you don't get blown away, little Piglet. You'd be missed. People would say 'Where's little Piglet been blown to?'—really wanting to know. Well, good-bye. And thank you for happening to pass me."

The House at Pooh Corner

The more it snows
    (Tiddely pom),
The more it goes
    (Tiddely pom),
The more it goes
    (Tiddely pom)
    On snowing.
And nobody knows
    (Tiddely pom),
How cold my toes
    (Tiddely pom),
How cold my toes
    (Tiddely pom),
    Are growing.

The House at Pooh Corner

"I don't think Roo had better come," he said. "Not to-day."

"Why not?" said Roo, who wasn't supposed to be listening.

"Nasty cold day," said Rabbit, shaking his head. "And you were coughing this morning."

"How do you know?" asked Roo indignantly.

"Oh, Roo, you never told me," said Kanga reproachfully.

"It was a biscuit cough," said Roo, "not one you tell about."

The House at Pooh Corner

The wind had dropped, and the snow, tired of rushing round in circles trying to catch itself up, now fluttered gently down until it found a place on which to rest, and sometimes the place was Pooh's nose and sometimes it wasn't, and in a little while Piglet was wearing a white muffler round his neck and feeling more snowy behind the ears than he had ever felt before.

The House at Pooh Corner

If I were a bear,
    And a big bear too,
I shouldn't much care
    If it froze or snew;
I shouldn't much mind
    If it snowed or friz –
I'd be all fur-lined
    With a coat like his!

Now We Are Six

In a very little time they got to the corner of the field by the side of the pine-wood, where Eeyore's house wasn't any longer.

"There!" said Eeyore. "Not a stick of it left! Of course, I've still got this snow to do what I like with. One mustn't complain."

The House at Pooh Corner

Christopher Robin had spent the morning indoors going to Africa and back, and he had just got off the boat and was wondering what it was like outside, when who should come knocking at the door but Eeyore.

"Hallo, Eeyore," said Christopher Robin, as he opened the door and came out. "How are *you*?"

"It's snowing still," said Eeyore gloomily.

"So it is."

"*And* freezing."

"Is it?"

"Yes," said Eeyore. "However," he said, brightening up a little, "we haven't had an earthquake lately."

The House at Pooh Corner

READY FOR ANYTHING

*In which we find Quotations
about Journeys, Searches,
Adventures and Expotitions*

Christopher Robin was sitting outside his door, putting on his Big Boots. As soon as he saw the Big Boots, Pooh knew that an Adventure was going to happen, and he brushed the honey off his nose with the back of his paw, and spruced himself up as well as he could, so as to look Ready for Anything.

Winnie-the-Pooh

James went a journey with the
  goat's new compass
    And he reached the end of
              his brick.

When We Were Very Young

"We are all going on an Expedition," said Christopher Robin, as he got up and brushed himself. "Thank you, Pooh."

"Going on an Expotition?" said Pooh eagerly. "I don't think I've ever been on one of those. Where are we going to on this Expotition?"

"Expedition, silly old Bear. It's got an 'x' in it."

"Oh!" said Pooh. "I know." But he didn't really.

Winnie-the-Pooh

"It is because you are a very small animal that you will be Useful in the adventure before us."

Winnie-the-Pooh

"Christopher Robin and I are going for a Short Walk," he said, "not a Jostle. If he likes to bring Pooh and Piglet with him, I shall be glad of their company, but one must be able to Breathe."

The House at Pooh Corner

"Where are we going?" said Pooh, hurrying after him, and wondering whether it was to be an Explore or a What-shall-I-do-about-you-know-what.

"Nowhere," said Christopher Robin.

The House at Pooh Corner

James James
Morrison Morrison
Weatherby George Dupree
Took great
Care of his Mother,
Though he was only three.
James James
Said to his Mother,
"Mother," he said, said he;
"You must never go down to the
end of the town, if you don't go
down with me."

When We Were Very Young

"We're all going on an Expotition with Christopher Robin!"

"What is it when we're on it?"

"A sort of boat, I think," said Pooh.

"Oh! that sort."

"Yes. And we're going to discover a Pole or something. Or was it a Mole? Anyhow we're going to discover it."

Winnie-the-Pooh

"We're going to discover the North Pole."

"Oh!" said Pooh again. "What *is* the North Pole?" he asked.

"It's just a thing you discover," said Christopher Robin carelessly, not being quite sure himself.

"Oh! I see," said Pooh. "Are bears any good at discovering it?"

"Of course they are. And Rabbit and Kanga and all of you. It's an Expedition. That's what an Expedition means. A long line of everybody. You'd better tell the others to get ready, while I see if my gun's all right."

Winnie-the-Pooh

As soon as Rabbit was out of sight, Pooh remembered that he had forgotten to ask who Small was, and whether he was the sort of friend-and-relation who settled on one's nose, or the sort who got trodden on by mistake, and as it was Too Late Now, he thought he would begin the Hunt by looking for Piglet, and asking him what they were looking for before he looked for it.

The House at Pooh Corner

"Hallo!" said Piglet, "what are *you* doing?"

"Hunting," said Pooh.

"Hunting what?"

"Tracking something," said Winnie-the-Pooh very mysteriously.

"Tracking what?" said Piglet, coming closer.

"That's just what I ask myself. I ask myself, What?"

"What do you think you'll answer?"

"I shall have to wait until I catch up with it," said Winnie-the-Pooh.

Winnie-the-Pooh

"We must rescue him at once! I thought he was with *you*, Pooh. Owl, could you rescue him on your back?"

"I don't think so," said Owl, after grave thought. "It is doubtful if the necessary dorsal muscles—"

"Then would you fly to him at *once* and say that Rescue is Coming? And Pooh and I will think of a Rescue and come as quick as ever we can. Oh, don't *talk*, Owl, go on quick!" And, still thinking of something to say, Owl flew off.

Winnie-the-Pooh

When I am in my ship, I see
   The other ships go sailing by.
A sailor leans and calls to me
   As his tall ship goes sailing by.
Across the sea he leans to me,

Above the wind I hear him cry:
"Is this the way to Round-the-
   World?"
He calls as he goes by.

When We Were Very Young

"Pooh," he said, "where did you find that pole?"

Pooh looked at the pole in his hands.

"I just found it," he said. "I thought it ought to be useful. I just picked it up."

"Pooh," said Christopher Robin solemnly, "the Expedition is over. You have found the North Pole!"

"Oh!" said Pooh.

Winnie-the-Pooh

When I go up the Amazon,
I stop at night and fire a gun
  To call my faithful band.
And Indians in twos and threes,
Come silently between the trees,
  And wait for me to land.
And if I do not want to play
With any Indians to-day,
  I simply wave my hand.
And then they turn and go away –
  They always understand.

When We Were Very Young

"Pooh's found the North Pole," said Christopher Robin. "Isn't that lovely?"

Pooh looked modestly down.

"Is that it?" said Eeyore.

"Yes," said Christopher Robin.

"Is that what we were looking for?"

"Yes," said Pooh.

"Oh!" said Eeyore. "Well, anyhow – it didn't rain," he said.

Winnie-the-Pooh

"It's a funny thing," said Rabbit ten minutes later, "how everything looks the same in a mist. Have you noticed it, Pooh?"

Pooh said that he had.

"Lucky we know the Forest so well, or we might get lost," said Rabbit half an hour later, and he gave the careless laugh which you give when you know the Forest so well that you can't get lost.

The House at Pooh Corner

"We'll take him to the North Pole," said Rabbit. "because it was a very long explore finding it, so it will be a very long explore for Tigger un-finding it again."

It was now Pooh's turn to feel very glad, because it was he who had first found the North Pole, and when they got there, Tigger would see a notice which said, "Discovered by Pooh, Pooh found it," and then Tigger would know, which perhaps he didn't now, the sort of Bear Pooh was. *That* sort of Bear."

The House at Pooh Corner

A THOUGHTFUL
SPOT

*In which we find Quotations
about Thinking
and Thoughts*

Half-way between Pooh's house and Piglet's house was a Thoughtful Spot where they met sometimes when they had decided to go and see each other, and as it was warm and out of the wind they would sit down there for a little and wonder what they would do now that they *had* seen each other. One day when they had decided not to do anything, Pooh made up a verse about it, so that everybody should know what the place was for.

This warm and sunny Spot
    Belongs to Pooh.
And here he wonders what
    He's going to do.
Oh, bother, I forgot –
    It's Piglet's too.

The House at Pooh Corner

It's a very funny thought that, if
    Bears were Bees,
They'd build their nests at the
    bottom of trees.
And that being so (if the Bees were
    Bears),
We shouldn't have to climb up all
    these stairs.

Winnie-the-Pooh

"He's out," said Pooh sadly. "That's what it is. He's not in. I shall have to go a fast Thinking Walk by myself. Bother!"

The House at Pooh Corner

... last week when Christopher Robin said to me, "What about that story you were going to tell me about what happened to Pooh when—" I happened to say very quickly, "What about nine times a hundred and seven?" And when we had done that one, we had one about cows going through a gate at two a minute, and there are three hundred in the field, so how many are left after an hour and a half? We find these very exciting, and when we have been excited quite enough, we curl up and go to sleep ... and Pooh, sitting wakeful a little longer on his chair by our pillow, thinks Grand Thoughts to himself about Nothing, until he, too, closes his eyes and nods his head, and follows us on tiptoe into the Forest.

The House at Pooh Corner

The Old Grey Donkey, Eeyore, stood by himself in a thistly corner of the Forest, his front feet well apart, his head on one side, and thought about things. Sometimes he thought sadly to himself, "Why?" and sometimes he thought, "Wherefore?" and sometimes he thought, "Inasmuch as which?" – and sometimes he didn't quite know what he *was* thinking about.

Winnie-the-Pooh

Here is Edward Bear, coming downstairs now, bump, bump, bump, on the back of his head, behind Christopher Robin. It is, as far as he knows, the only way of coming downstairs, but sometimes he feels that there really is another way, if only he could stop bumping for a moment and think of it. And then he feels that perhaps there isn't.

Winnie-the-Pooh

If I were John and John were Me,
Then he'd be six and I'd be three.
If John were Me and I were John,
I shouldn't have these trousers on.

Now We Are Six

41

"Well, we must be getting home," said Kanga. "Good-bye, Pooh." And in three large jumps she was gone.

Pooh looked after her as she went.

"I wish I could jump like that," he thought. "Some can and some can't. That's how it is."

Winnie-the-Pooh

Often, when he had a long walk home through the Forest, he had wished that he were a bird; but now he thought jerkily to himself at the bottom of Kanga's pocket,

    this
"If   is   shall
           flying   I
           take
    really   to
never   it."

Winnie-the-Pooh

"Owl," said Rabbit shortly, "you and I have brains. The others have fluff. If there is any thinking to be done in this Forest – and when I say thinking I mean *thinking* – you and I must do it."

"Yes," said Owl. "I was."

The House at Pooh Corner

Piglet wasn't listening, he was so agog at the thought of seeing Christopher Robin's blue braces again. He had only seen them once before, when he was much younger, and, being a little over-excited by them, had had to go to bed half an hour earlier than usual; and he had always wondered since if they were *really* as blue and as bracing as he had thought them.

The House at Pooh Corner

"Come on, Tigger," he called out. "It's easy."

But Tigger was holding on to the branch and saying to himself: "It's all very well for Jumping Animals like Kangas, but it's quite different for Swimming Animals like Tiggers." And he thought of himself floating on his back down a river, or striking out from one island to another, and he felt that that was really the life for a Tigger.

The House at Pooh Corner

Halfway up the stairs
Isn't up,
And isn't down.
It isn't in the nursery,
It isn't in the town.
And all sorts of funny thoughts
Run round my head:
  "It isn't really
Anywhere!
It's somewhere else
Instead!"

When We Were Very Young

He came to Owl's door, and he knocked and he rang, and he rang and he knocked, and at last Owl's head came out and said "Go away, I'm thinking – oh, it's you?" which was how he always began.

The House at Pooh Corner

"I think—" began Piglet nervously.

"Don't," said Eeyore.

"I think *Violets* are rather nice," said Piglet. And he laid his bunch in front of Eeyore and scampered off.

The House at Pooh Corner

"Supposing a tree feel down, Pooh, when we were underneath it?"

"Supposing it didn't," said Pooh after careful thought.

The House at Pooh Corner

"I have just been thinking, and I have come to a very important decision. *These are the wrong sort of bees*."

"Are they?"

"Quite the wrong sort. So I should think they would make the wrong sort of honey, shouldn't you?"

Winnie-the-Pooh

BANG!!!???***!!!

Piglet lay there, wondering what had happened. At first he thought that the whole world had blown up; and then he thought that perhaps only the Forest part of it had; and then he thought that perhaps only *he* had, and he was now alone in the moon or somewhere, and would never see Christopher Robin or Pooh or Eeyore again. And then he thought, "Well, even if I'm in the moon, I needn't be face downwards all the time," so he got cautiously up and looked about him.

He was still in the Forest!

Winnie-the-Pooh

When you are a Bear of Very Little Brain, and you Think of Things, you find sometimes that a Thing which seemed very Thingish inside you is quite different when it gets out into the open and has other people looking at it.

The House at Pooh Corner

"I'm very glad," said Pooh happily, "that I thought of giving you a Useful Pot to put things in."

"I'm very glad," said Piglet happily, "that I thought of giving you Something to put in a Useful Pot."

But Eeyore wasn't listening. He was taking the balloon out, and putting it back again, as happy as could be. . . .

Winnie-the-Pooh

Then he began to think of all the things Christopher Robin would want to tell him when he came back from wherever he was going to, and how muddling it would be for a Bear of Very Little Brain to try and get them right in his mind. "So, perhaps," he said sadly to himself, "Christopher Robin won't tell me any more," and he wondered if being a Faithful Knight meant that you just went on being faithful without being told things.

The House at Pooh Corner

"When you wake up in the morning, Pooh," said Piglet at last, "what's the first thing you say to yourself?"

"What's for breakfast?" said Pooh. "What do *you* say, Piglet?"

"I say, I wonder what's going to happen exciting *to-day*?" said Piglet.

Pooh nodded thoughtfully.

"It's the same thing," he said.

Winnie-the-Pooh

A GOOD HUM

*In which we find Quotations
about Poetry, Songs
and Hums*

"Did you make that song up?"

"Well, I sort of made it up," said Pooh. "It isn't Brain," he went on humbly, "because You Know Why, Rabbit; but it comes to me sometimes."

"Ah!" said Rabbit, who never let things come to him, but always went and fetched them.

The House at Pooh Corner

. . . he jumped up and down to keep warm, and a hum came suddenly into his head, which seemed to him a Good Hum, such as is Hummed Hopefully to Others.

The House at Pooh Corner

"Oh Kanga," said Pooh . . . "I don't know if you are interested in Poetry at all?"

"Hardly at all," said Kanga.

"Oh!" said Pooh.

Winnie-the-Pooh

But whatever his weight in pounds, shillings, and ounces,
He always seems bigger because of his bounces.

"And that's the whole poem," he said. "Do you like it, Piglet?"

"All except the shillings," said Piglet. "I don't think they ought to be there."

"They wanted to come in after the pounds," explained Pooh, "so I let them. It is the best way to write poetry, letting things come."

"Oh, I didn't know," said Piglet.

The House at Pooh Corner

"But it isn't Easy," sad Pooh to himself, as he looked at what had once been Owl's House. "Because Poetry and Hums aren't things which you get, they're things which get *you*. And all you can do is to go where they can find you."

The House at Pooh Corner

"*The more it snows, tiddely pom—*"

"Tiddely what?" said Piglet.

"Pom," said Pooh. "I put that in to make it more hummy. *The more it goes, tiddely pom, the more—*"

"Didn't you say snows?"

"Yes, but that was *before*."

"Before the tiddely pom?"

"It was a *different* tiddely pom." said Pooh, feeling rather muddled now.

The House at Pooh Corner

"Talking of Poetry," said Pooh, "I made up a little piece as I was coming along. It went like this. Er – now let me see—"

"Fancy!" said Kanga. "Now Roo, dear—"

"You'll like this piece of poetry," said Rabbit.

"You'll love it," said Piglet.

"You must listen very carefully," said Rabbit.

"So as not to miss any of it," said Piglet.

Winnie-the-Pooh

"Pooh," he said at last, and a little timidly, because he didn't want Pooh to think he was Giving In, "I was just wondering. How would it be if we went home now and *practised* your song, and then sang it to Eeyore to-morrow – or – or the next day, when we happen to see him?"

"That's a very good idea, Piglet," said Pooh. "We'll practise it now as we go along. But it's no good going home to practise it, because it's a special Outdoor Song which has To Be Sung In The Snow."

The House at Pooh Corner

And nobody
KNOWS-tiddely-pom,
How cold my
TOES-tiddely-pom
How cold my
TOES-tiddely-pom
Are
Growing.

He sang it like that, which is much the best way of singing it, and when he had finished, he waited for Piglet to say that, of all the Outdoor Hums for Snowy Weather he had ever heard, this was the best. And, after thinking the matter out carefully, Piglet said:

"Pooh," he said solemnly, "it isn't the *toes* so much as the *ears*."

The House at Pooh Corner

I could spend a happy morning
  Seeing Piglet.
And I couldn't spend a happy
  morning
  Not seeing Piglet.
And it doesn't seem to matter
If I don't see Owl and Eeyore (or
  any of the others),
And I'm not going to see Owl or
  Eeyore (or any of the others)
  Or Christopher Robin.

Written down like this, it doesn't seem a very good song, but coming through pale fawn fluff at about half-past eleven on a very sunny morning, it seemed to Pooh to be one of the best songs he had ever sung. So he went on singing it.

The House at Pooh Corner

One day, when Pooh was walking towards this bridge, he was trying to make up a piece of poetry about fircones, because there they were, lying about on each side of him, and he felt singy. So he picked a fir-cone up, and looked at it, and said to himself, "This is a very good fir-cone, and something ought to rhyme to it." But he couldn't think of anything. And then this came into his head suddenly:

Here is a myst'ry
About a little fir-tree.
Owl says it's *his* tree,
And Kanga says it's *her* tree.

"Which doesn't make sense," said Pooh, "because Kanga doesn't live in a tree."

The House at Pooh Corner

Cottleston, Cottleston, Cottleston
  Pie.
A fly can't bird, but a bird can fly.
Ask me a riddle and I reply:
"*Cottleston, Cottleston, Cottleston
  Pie.*"

That was the first verse. When he had finished it, Eeyore didn't actually say that he didn't like it, so Pooh very kindly sang the second verse to him.

Winnie-the-Pooh

47

"I shall sing that first line twice, and perhaps if I sing it very quickly, I shall find myself singing the third and fourth lines before I have time to think of them, and that will be a Good Song. Now then:"

Winnie-the-Pooh

Pooh followed slowly. He had something better to do than to find a new house for Owl; he had to make up a Pooh song about the old one. Because he had promised Piglet days and days ago that he would, and whenever he and Piglet had met since, Piglet didn't actually say anything, but you knew at once why he didn't; and if anybody mentioned Hums or Trees or String or Storms-in-the-Night, Piglet's nose went all pink at the tip, and he talked about something quite different in a hurried sort of way.

The House at Pooh Corner

. . . they all sang the Outdoor Song for Snowy Weather the rest of the way home, Piglet, who was still not quite sure of his voice, putting in the tiddely-poms again.

"And I know it *seems* easy," said Piglet to himself, "but it isn't *every one* who could do it."

The House at Pooh Corner

He coughed in an important way, and began again: "What-nots and Etceteras, before I begin, or perhaps I should say, before I end, I have a piece of Poetry to read to you. Hitherto – hitherto – a long word meaning – well, you'll see what it means directly – hitherto, as I was saying, all the Poetry in the Forest has been written by Pooh, a Bear with a Pleasing Manner but a Positively Startling Lack of Brain. The Poem which I am now about to read to you was written by Eeyore, or Myself, in a Quiet Moment. If somebody will take Roo's bull's eye away from him, and wake up Owl, we shall all be able to enjoy it. I call it – POEM."

The House at Pooh Corner

"This is the first verse," he said to Piglet, when he was ready with it.

"First verse of what?"

"My song."

"What song?"

"This one."

"Which one?"

"Well, if you listen, Piglet, you'll hear it."

"How do you know I'm not listening?"

Pooh couldn't answer that one, so he began to sing.

Winnie-the-Pooh

CRUSTIMONEY
PROSEEDCAKE

*In which we find Quotations
about Important Things to be Done and
How to Organize Others to Do Them*

"Well," said Owl, "the customary procedure in such cases is as follows."

"What does Crustimoney Proseedcake mean?" said Pooh. "For I am a Bear of Very Little Brain, and long words Bother me."

"It means the Thing to Do."

"As long as it means that, I don't mind," said Pooh humbly.

Winnie-the-Pooh

"I'm not going to do Nothing any more."

"Never again?"

"Well, not so much. They don't let you."

The House at Pooh Corner

"Well," said Pooh, "at eleven o'clock – at eleven o'clock – well, at eleven o'clock, you see, I generally get home about then. Because I have One or Two Things to Do."

The House at Pooh Corner

It was going to be one of Rabbit's busy days. As soon as he woke up he felt important, as if everything depended upon him. It was just the day for Organizing Something, or for Writing a Notice Signed Rabbit, or for Seeing What Everybody Else Thought About It. It was a perfect morning for hurrying round to Pooh, and saying, "Very well, then, I'll tell Piglet," and then going to Piglet, and saying, "Pooh thinks – but perhaps I'd better see Owl first." It was a Captainish sort of day, when everybody said, "Yes, Rabbit" and "No, Rabbit," and waited until he had told them.

The House at Pooh Corner

49

"Now," said Rabbit, "this is a Search, and I've Organized it—"

"Done what to it?" said Pooh.

"Organized it. Which means – well, it's what you do to a Search, when you don't all look in the same place at once. So I want *you*, Pooh, to search by the Six Pine Trees first, and then work your way towards Owl's House, and look out for me there. Do you see?"

"No," said Pooh. "What—"

"Then I'll see you at Owl's House in about an hour's time."

"Is Piglet organdized too?"

"We all are," said Rabbit, and off he went.

The House at Pooh Corner

"I *think* that I have just remembered something. I have just remembered something that I forgot to do yesterday and sha'n't be able to do to-morrow. So I suppose I really ought to go back and do it now."

"We'll do it this afternoon, and I'll come with you," said Pooh.

"It isn't the sort of thing you can do in the afternoon," said Piglet quickly. "It's a very particular morning thing, that has to be done in the morning, and, if possible, between the hours of—What would you say the time was?"

"About twelve," said Winnie-the-Pooh, looking at the sun.

"Between, as I was saying, the hours of twelve and twelve five. So, really, dear old Pooh, if you'll excuse me—"

Winnie-the-Pooh

"Now it happened that Kanga had felt rather motherly that morning, and Wanting to Count Things – like Roo's vests, and how many pieces of soap there were left, and the two clean spots in Tigger's feeder; so she had sent them out with a packet of watercress sandwiches for Roo and a packet of extract-of-malt sandwiches for Tigger, to have a nice long morning in the Forest not getting into mischief.

The House at Pooh Corner

Rabbit began to feel that it was time he took command.

"Now, Pooh," he said, "when I say 'Now!' you can drop it. Eeyore, when I say 'Now!' Pooh will drop his stone."

"Thank you very much, Rabbit, but I expect I shall know."

The House at Pooh Corner

"We've come to wish you a Very Happy Thursday," said Pooh, when he had gone in and out once or twice just to make sure that he *could* get out again.

"Why, what's going to happen on Thursday?" asked Rabbit, and when Pooh had explained, and Rabbit, whose life was made up of Important Things, said, "Oh, I thought you'd really come about something,".

The House at Pooh Corner

MY
MISTAKE
AGAIN

In which we find Quotations about Misunderstandings

"Hallo, Piglet," he said. "I thought you were out."

"No," said Piglet, "it's you who were out, Pooh."

"So it was," said Pooh. "I knew one of us was."

The House at Pooh Corner

"Kanga, I see that the time has come to speak plainly."

"Funny little Roo," said Kanga, as she got the bath-water ready.

"I am *not* Roo," said Piglet loudly. "I am Piglet!"

"Yes, dear, yes," said Kanga soothingly. "And imitating Piglet's voice too! So clever of him,"

"Can't you *see?*" shouted Piglet. "Haven't you got *eyes? Look* at me!"

"I *am* looking, Roo, dear," said Kanga rather severely. "And you know what I told you yesterday about making faces. If you go on making faces like Piglet's, you will grow up to *look* like Piglet – and *then* think how sorry you will be."

Winnie-the-Pooh

"The thing to do is as follows. First, Issue a Reward. Then—"

"Just a moment," said Pooh, holding up his paw. "*What* do we do to this – what you were saying? You sneezed just as you were going to tell me."

"I *didn't* sneeze."

"Yes, you did, Owl."

"Excuse me, Pooh, I didn't. You can't sneeze without knowing it."

"Well, you can't know it without something having been sneezed."

Winnie-the-Pooh

"Owl," said Pooh, "I have thought of something."

"Astute and Helpful Bear," said Owl.

Pooh looked proud at being called a stout and helpful bear, and said modestly that he just happened to think of it.

Winnie-the-Pooh

51

"Handsome bell-rope, isn't it?" said Owl.

Pooh nodded.

"It reminds me of something," he said, "but I can't think what. Where did you get it?"

"I just came across it in the Forest. It was hanging over a bush, and I thought at first somebody lived there, so I rang it, and nothing happened, and then I rang it again very loudly, and it came off in my hand, and as nobody seemed to want it, I took it home, and—"

"Owl," said Pooh solemnly, "you made a mistake. Somebody did want it."

"Who?"

"Eeyore. My dear friend Eeyore. He was – he was fond of it."

"Fond of it?"

"Attached to it," said Winnie-the-Pooh sadly.

Winnie-the-Pooh

52

"Pooh!" he cried. "I believe it's Tigger and Roo!"

"So it is," said Pooh. "I thought it was a Jagular and another Jagular."

The House at Pooh Corner

"Excuse me a moment, but there's something climbing up your table," and with one loud *Worraworraworraworraworra* he jumped at the end of the tablecloth, pulled it to the ground, wrapped himself up in it three times, rolled to the other end of the room, and, after a terrible struggle, got his head into the daylight again, and said cheerfully: "Have I won?"

"That's my tablecloth," said Pooh, as he began to unwind Tigger.

"I wondered what it was," said Tigger.

"It goes on the table and you put things on it."

"Then why did it try to bite me when I wasn't looking?"

"I don't *think* it did," said Pooh.

"It tried," said Tigger, "but I was too quick for it."

The House at Pooh Corner

Before he knew where he was, Piglet was in the bath, and Kanga was scrubbing him firmly with a large lathery flannel.

"*Ow!*" cried Piglet. "Let me out! I'm Piglet!"

"Don't open the mouth, dear, or the soap goes in," said Kanga. "There! What did I tell you?"

"You – you – you – did it on purpose," spluttered Piglet, as soon as he could speak again ... and then accidentally had another mouthful of lathery flannel.

Winnie-the-Pooh

"It's just the place," he explained, "for an Ambush."

"What sort of bush?" whispered Pooh to Piglet. "A gorse-bush?"

"My dear Pooh," said Owl in his superior way, "don't you know what an Ambush is?"

"Owl," said Piglet, looking round at him severely, "Pooh's whisper was a perfectly private whisper, and there was no need—"

"An Ambush," said Owl, "is a sort of Surprise."

"So is a gorse-bush sometimes," said Pooh.

Winnie-the-Pooh

"You bounced me," said Eeyore gruffly.

"I didn't really. I had a cough, and I happened to be behind Eeyore, and I said '*Grrrr – oppp – ptschschschz*'"

The House at Pooh Corner

"Come on," said Rabbit. "I know it's this way."

They went on. Ten minutes later they stopped again.

"It's very silly," said Rabbit, "but just for the moment I—Ah, of course. Come on." . . .

"Here we are," said Rabbit ten minutes later. "No, we're not." . . .

"Now," said Rabbit ten minutes later, "I think we ought to be getting – or are we a little bit more to the right than I thought?" . . .

The House at Pooh Corner

"All I did was I coughed," said Tigger.

"He bounced," said Eeyore.

"Well, I sort of boffed," said Tigger.

The House at Pooh Corner

Piglet looked up, and looked away again. And he felt so Foolish and Uncomfortable that he had almost decided to run away to Sea and be a Sailor.

The House at Pooh Corner

"Hallo, Pooh. Thank you for asking, but I shall be able to use it again in a day or two."

"Use what?" said Pooh.

"What we are talking about."

"I wasn't talking about anything," said Pooh, looking puzzled.

"My mistake again. I thought you were saying how sorry you were about my tail, being all numb, and could you do anything to help?"

"No," said Pooh. "That wasn't me," he said. He thought for a little and then suggested helpfully: "Perhaps it was somebody else."

"Well, thank him for me when you see him."

Winnie-the-Pooh

"What's Eeyore talking about?" Piglet whispered to Pooh.

"I don't know," said Pooh rather dolefully.

"I thought this was *your* party."

"I thought it was *once*. But I suppose it isn't."

"I'd sooner it was yours than Eeyore's," said Piglet.

"So would I," said Pooh.

Winnie-the-Pooh

"Pooh," said Owl severely, "did *you* do that?"

"No," said Pooh humbly. "I don't *think* so."

"Then who did?"

"I think it was the wind," said Piglet. "I think your house has blown down."

"Oh, is that it? I thought it was Pooh."

"No," said Pooh.

The House at Pooh Corner

So she got cross with Owl and said that his house was a Disgrace, all damp and dirty, and it was quite time it did tumble down. Look at that horrid bunch of toadstools growing out of the corner there? So Owl looked down, a little surprised because he didn't know about this, and then gave a short sarcastic laugh, and explained that this was his sponge, and that if people didn't know a perfectly ordinary bath-sponge when they saw it, things were coming to a pretty pass.

The House at Pooh Corner

Then Piglet saw what a Foolish Piglet he had been, and he was so ashamed of himself that he ran straight off home and went to bed with a headache.

Winnie-the-Pooh

"If it was the wind," said Owl, considering the matter, "then it wasn't Pooh's fault. No blame can be attached to him." With these kind words he flew up to look at his new ceiling. .

"Piglet!" called Pooh in a loud whisper.

Piglet leant down to him.

"Yes, Pooh?"

"*What* did he say was attached to me?"

"He said he didn't blame you."

"Oh! I thought he meant – Oh, I see."

The House at Pooh Corner

"It's coming!" said Pooh.

"Are you *sure* it's mine?" squeaked Piglet excitedly.

"Yes, because it's grey. A big grey one. Here it comes! A very – big – grey —Oh, no, it isn't, it's Eeyore."

And out floated Eeyore.

The House at Pooh Corner

"What are *you* trying to do?"

"I was trying to reach the knocker," said Piglet. "I just came round—"

"Let me do it for you," said Pooh kindly. So he reached up and knocked at the door. "I have just seen Eeyore," he began, "and poor Eeyore is in a Very Sad Condition, because it's his birthday, and nobody has taken any notice of it, and he's very Gloomy – you know what Eeyore is – and there he was, and—What a long time whoever lives here is answering this door." And he knocked again.

"But Pooh," said Piglet, "it's your own house!"

"Oh!" said Pooh. "So it is," he said. "Well, let's go in."

Winnie-the-Pooh

Kanga was down below tying the things on, and calling out to Owl, "You won't want this dirty old dish-cloth any more, will you, and what about this carpet, it's all in holes," and Owl was calling back indignantly, "Of course I do! It's just a question of arranging the furniture properly, and it isn't a dishcloth, it's my shawl."

The House at Pooh Corner

"Is it a very Grand thing to be an Afternoon, what you said?"

"A what?" said Christopher Robin lazily, as he listened to something else.

"On a horse?" explained Pooh.

"A Knight?"

"Oh, was that it?" said Pooh. "I thought it was a—Is it as Grand as a King and Factors and all the other things you said?"

"Well, it's not as grand as a King," said Christopher Robin, and then, as Pooh seemed disappointed, he added quickly, "but it's grander than Factors."

"Could a Bear be one?"

"Of course he could!" said Christopher Robin. "I'll make you one." And he took a stick and touched Pooh on the shoulder, and said, "Rise, Sir Pooh de Bear, most faithful of all my Knights."

The House at Pooh Corner

ANIMALS OF
HOSTILE INTENT

*In which we find Quotations about such
Strange Creatures as Heffalumps,
Woozles, Wizzles, Jagulars and
Spotted or Herbaceous Backsons*

"Look, Pooh!" said Piglet suddenly. "There's something in one of the Pine Trees."

"So there is!" said Pooh, looking up wonderingly. "There's an Animal."

Piglet took Pooh's arm, in case Pooh was frightened.

"Is it One of the Fiercer Animals?" he said, looking the other way.

Pooh nodded.

"It's a Jagular," he said.

"What do Jagulars do?" asked Piglet, hoping that they wouldn't.

"They hide in the branches of trees, and drop on you as you go underneath," said Pooh. "Christopher Robin told me."

"Perhaps we better hadn't go underneath, Pooh. In case he dropped and hurt himself."

"They don't hurt themselves," said Pooh. "They're such very good droppers."

The House at Pooh Corner

"Now, look there." He pointed to the ground in front of him. "What do you see there?"

"Tracks," said Piglet. "Pawmarks." He gave a little squeak of excitement. "Oh, Pooh! Do you think it's a – a – a Woozle?"

"It may be," said Pooh. "Sometimes it is, and sometimes it isn't. You never can tell with pawmarks."

Winnie-the-Pooh

But he didn't look round, because if you look round and see a Very Fierce Heffalump looking down at you, sometimes you forget what you were going to say.

The House at Pooh Corner

57

"What's the matter?" asked Piglet.

"It's a very funny thing," said Bear, "but there seem to be *two* animals now. This – whatever-it-was – has been joined by another – whatever-it-is – and the two of them are now proceeding in company. Would you mind coming with me, Piglet, in case they turn out to be Hostile Animals?"

Piglet scratched his ear in a nice sort of way, and said that he had nothing to do until Friday, and would be delighted to come, in case it really *was* a Woozle.

"You mean, in case it really is two Woozles," said Winnie-the-Pooh, and Piglet said that anyhow he had nothing to do until Friday. So off they went together.

Winnie-the-Pooh

One day, when Christopher Robin and Winnie-the-Pooh and Piglet were all talking together, Christopher Robin finished the mouthful he was eating and said carelessly: "I saw a Heffalump to-day, Piglet."

"What was it doing?" asked Piglet.

"Just lumping along," said Christopher Robin. "I don't think it saw *me*."

"I saw one once," said Piglet. "At least, I think I did," he said. "Only perhaps it wasn't."

"So did I," said Pooh, wondering what a Heffalump was like.

"You don't often see them," said Christopher Robin carelessly.

"Not now," said Piglet.

"Not at this time of year," said Pooh.

Winnie-the-Pooh

Ernest was an elephant, a great big fellow,
Leonard was a lion with a six-foot tail,
George was a goat, and his beard was yellow,
And James was a very small snail.

When We Were Very Young

... as they came to the Six Pine Trees, Pooh looked round to see that nobody else was listening, and said in a very solemn voice:

"Piglet, I have decided something."

"What have you decided, Pooh?"

"I have decided to catch a Heffalump."

Pooh nodded his head several times as he said this, and waited for Piglet to say "How?" or "Pooh, you couldn't!" or something helpful of that sort, but Piglet said nothing. The fact was Piglet was wishing that *he* had thought about it first.

Winnie-the-Pooh

So they went on, feeling just a little anxious now, in case the three animals in front of them were of Hostile Intent. And Piglet wished very much that his Grandfather T. W. were there, instead of elsewhere, and Pooh thought how nice it would be if they met Christopher Robin suddenly but quite accidentally, and only because he liked Christopher Robin so much.

Winnie-the-Pooh

Piglet was so excited at the idea of being Useful that he forgot to be frightened any more, and when Rabbit went on to say that Kangas were only Fierce during the winter months, being at other times of an Affectionate Disposition, he could hardly sit still, he was so eager to begin being useful at once.

Winnie-the-Pooh

"The tracks!" said Pooh. "*A third animal has joined the other two!*"

"Pooh!" cried Piglet. "Do you think it is another Woozle?"

"No," said Pooh, "because it makes different marks. It is either Two Woozles and one, as it might be, Wizzle, or Two, as it might be, Wizzles and one, if so it is, Woozle."

Winnie-the-Pooh

"Well, good night, Pooh," said Piglet, when they had got to Pooh's house. "And we meet at six o'clock to-morrow morning by the Pine Trees, and see how many Heffalumps we've got in our Trap."

"Six o'clock, Piglet. And have you got any string?"

"No. Why do you want string?"

"To lead them home with."

"Oh! ... I *think* Heffalumps come if you whistle."

"Some do and some don't. You never can tell with Heffalumps. Well, good night!"

"Good night!"

Winnie-the-Pooh

59

"Let's look for dragons," I said to
  Pooh.
"Yes, let's," said Pooh to Me
We crossed the river and a found a
  few –
"Yes, those are dragons all right,"
  said Pooh.
"As soon as I saw their beaks I
  knew.
That's what they are," said Pooh,
  said he.
"That's what they are," said Pooh.

"Let's frighten the dragons," I said
  to Pooh.
"That's right," said Pooh to Me.
"*I'm* not afraid," I said to Pooh,
And I held his paw and I shouted
  "Shoo!
Silly old dragons!" – and off they
  flew.
"I wasn't afraid," said Pooh, said
  he,
"I'm *never* afraid with you."

Now We Are Six

"There's just one thing,"
said Piglet, fidgeting a bit. "I was
talking to Christopher Robin, and
he said that a Kanga was Generally
Regarded as One of the Fiercer
Animals. I am not frightened of
Fierce Animals in the ordinary way,
but it is well known that if One of
the Fiercer Animals is Deprived of
Its Young, it becomes as fierce as
Two of the Fiercer Animals."

Winnie-the-Pooh

"Christopher Robin!" he
said in a loud whisper.
"Hallo!"
"I think the bees *suspect*
something!"
"What sort of thing?"
"I don't know. But something
tells me that they're *suspicious*!"
"Perhaps they think that you're
after their honey?"
"It may be that. You never can
tell with bees."

Winnie-the-Pooh

"*Worraworraworraworraworra*," said Whatever-it-was, and Pooh found that he wasn't asleep after all.

"What can it be?" he thought. "There are lots of noises in the Forest, but this is a different one. It isn't a growl, and it isn't a purr, and it isn't a bark, and it isn't the noise-you-make-before-beginning-a-piece-of-poetry, but it's a noise of some kind, made by a strange animal! And he's making it outside my door. So I shall get up and ask him not to do it."

The House at Pooh Corner

"Well," said Owl, "the Spotted or Herbaceous Backson is just a—"

"At least," he said, "it's really more of a—"

"Of course," he said, "it depends on the—"

"Well," said Owl, "the fact is," he said, "I don't know *what* they're like," said Owl frankly.

"Thank you," said Rabbit. And he hurried off to see Pooh.

The House at Pooh Corner

He got out of bed and opened his front door.

"Hallo!" said Pooh, in case there was anything outside.

"Hallo!" said Whatever-it-was.

"Oh!" said Pooh. "Hallo!"

"Hallo!"

"Oh, *there* you are!" said Pooh. "Hallo!"

"Hallo!" said the Strange Animal, wondering how long this was going on.

Pooh was just going to say "Hallo!" for the fourth time when he thought that he wouldn't, so he said, "Who is it?" instead.

"Me," said a voice.

"Oh!" said Pooh. "Well, come here."

So Whatever-it-was came here, and in the light of the candle he and Pooh looked at each other.

"I'm Pooh," said Pooh.

"I'm Tigger," said Tigger.

"Oh!" said Pooh, for he had never seen an animal like this before. "Does Christopher Robin know about you?"

"Of course he does," said Tigger.

The House at Pooh Corner

61

"Oh! Piglet," said Pooh excitedly, "we're going on an Expotition, all of us, with things to eat. To discover something."

"To discover what?" said Piglet anxioiusly.

"Oh! just something."

"Nothing fierce?"

"Christopher Robin didn't say anything about fierce. He just said it had an 'x'."

"It isn't their necks I mind," said Piglet earnestly. "It's their teeth. But if Christopher Robin is coming I don't mind anything."

Winnie-the-Pooh

Whenever I'm a shining Knight,
I buckle on my armour tight;
And then I look about for things,
Like Rushings-out, and Rescuings,
And Savings from the Dragon's
    Lair,
And fighting all the Dragons there.
And sometimes when our fights
    begin,
I think I'll let the Dragons win . . .
And then I think perhaps I won't,
Because they're Dragons, and I
    don't.

Now We Are Six

"Perhaps he's looking for a – for a—"

"A Spotted or Herbaceous Backson?"

"Yes," said Pooh. "One of those. In case it isn't."

Rabbit looked at him severely.

The House at Pooh Corner

"What happens when the Heffalump comes?" asked Piglet trembling, when he had heard the news.

"Perhaps he won't notice *you*, Piglet," said Pooh encouragingly, "because you're a Very Small Animal."

"But he'll notice *you*, Pooh."

"He'll notice *me*, and I shall notice *him*," said Pooh, thinking it out. "We'll notice each other for a long time, and then he'll say: 'Ho-*ho*!'"

Piglet shivered a little at the thought of that "Ho-*ho*!" and his ears began to twitch.

"W-what will *you* say?" he asked.

Pooh tried to think of something he would say, but the more he thought, the more he felt that there *is* no real answer to "Ho-*ho*!" said by a Heffalump in the sort of voice this Heffalump was going to say it in.

"I shan't say anything," said Pooh at last. "I shall just hum to myself, as if I was waiting for something."

The House at Pooh Corner

62

Whenever I walk in a London
   street,
I'm ever so careful to watch my
   feet;
And I keep in the squares,
And the masses of bears,
Who wait at the corners all ready
   to eat
The sillies who tread on the lines
   of the street,
Go back to their lairs,
And I say to them, "Bears,
Just look how I'm walking in all the
   squares!"

And the little bears growl to each
   other, "He's mine,
As soon as he's silly and steps on a
   line."
And some of the bigger bears try to
   pretend
That they came round the corner
   to look for a friend;
And they try to pretend that nobody
   cares
Whether you walk on the lines or
   squares.
But only the sillies believe their
   talk;
It's ever so portant how you walk.
And it's ever so jolly to
   call out, "Bears,
Just watch me walking in all the
   squares!"

When We Were Very Young

"Help, help!" cried Piglet, "a
Heffalump, a Horrible Heffa-
lump!" and he scampered off as
hard as he could, still crying out,
"Help! help, a Herrible Hoffalump!
Hoff, Hoff, a Hellible Horralump!
Holl, Holl, a Hoffable Hellerump!"
And he didn't stop crying and scam-
pering until he got to Christopher
Robin's house.

Winnie-the-Pooh

"Well, the point is, have you
seen a Spotted or Herbaceous
Backson in the Forest, at all?"
"No," said Pooh, "Not a – no,"
said Pooh. "I saw Tigger just now."
"That's no good."
"No," said Pooh. "I thought it
wasn't."
"Have you seen Piglet?"
"Yes," said Pooh. "I suppose *that*
isn't any good either?" he asked
meekly.
"Well, it depends if he saw
anything."
"He saw me," said Pooh.

The House at Pooh Corner

"Hallo, Pooh," said Piglet.
"Hallo, Piglet. This is Tigger."
"Oh, is it?" said Piglet, and he
edged round to the other side of
the table. "I thought Tiggers were
smaller than that."
"Not the big ones," said Tigger.

The House at Pooh Corner

IT'S HARD
TO BE BRAVE

In which we find Quotations
about Being
(and sometimes NOT being) Brave

"Piglet," said Rabbit, taking out a pencil, and licking the end of it, "you haven't any pluck."

"It is hard to be brave," said Piglet, sniffing slightly, "when you're only a Very Small Animal."

Winnie-the-Pooh

"They're always climbing trees like that," said Tigger. "Up and down all day."

"Oo, Tigger, are they *really*?"

"I'll show you," said Tigger bravely, "and you can sit on my back and watch me." For of all the things which he had said Tiggers could do, the only one he felt really certain about suddenly was climbing trees.

The House at Pooh Corner

Piglet nodded bravely at Pooh and said that it was a Very Clever pup-pup-pup Clever pup-pup Plan.

The House at Pooh Corner

Suddenly Winnie-the-Pooh stopped, and pointed excitedly in front of him. "*Look!*"

"*What?*" said Piglet, with a jump. And then, to show that he hadn't been frightened, he jumped up and down once or twice in an exercising sort of way.

Winnie-the-Pooh

"I just said 'Oh!'" said Piglet nervously. And so as to seem quite at ease he hummed tiddely-pom once or twice in a what-shall-we-do-now kind of way.

The House at Pooh Corner

"Then perhaps he'll say 'Ho-*ho*!' again?" suggested Piglet anxiously.

"He will," said Pooh.

Piglet's ears twitched so quickly that he had to lean them against the side of the Trap to keep them quiet.

The House at Pooh Corner

3 Cheers for Pooh!
(*For Who?*)
For Pooh –
(*Why what did he do?*)
I thought you knew;
He saved his friend from a wetting!
3 Cheers for Bear!
(*For where?*)
For Bear –
He couldn't swim,
But he rescued him!
(*He rescued who?*)
Oh, listen, do!
I am talking of Pooh –
(*Of who?*)
Of Pooh!
(*I'm sorry I keep forgetting*)

Winnie-the-Pooh

Binker's brave as lions when we're
    running in the park;
Binker's brave as tigers when we're
    lying in the dark;
Binker's brave as elephants. He
    never, never cries . . .
Except (like other people) when the
    soap gets in his eyes.

Now We Are Six

"It's a little Anxious," he said to himself, "to be a Very Small Animal Entirely Surrounded by Water. Christopher Robin and Pooh could escape by Climbing Trees, and Kanga could escape by Jumping, and Rabbit could escape by Burrowing, and Owl could escape by Flying, and Eeyore could escape by – by Making a Loud Noise Until Rescued, and here am I, surrounded by water and I can't do *anything*."

Winnie-the-Pooh

"It won't break," whispered Pooh comfortingly, "because you're a Small Animal, and I'll stand underneath, and if you save us all, it will be a Very Grand Thing to talk about afterwards, and perhaps I'll make up a Song, and people will say 'It was so grand what Piglet did that a Respectful Pooh Song was made about it!'"

The House at Pooh Corner

By and by Piglet woke up. As soon as he woke he said to himself, "Oh!" Then he said bravely, "Yes," and then, still more bravely, "Quite so." But he didn't feel very brave, for the word which was really jiggeting about in his brain was "Heffalumps."

What was a Heffalump like?

Was it Fierce?

Did it come when you whistled? And *how* did it come?

Was it Fond of Pigs at all?

If it was Fond of Pigs, did it make any difference *what sort of Pig*?

Supposing it was Fierce with Pigs, would it make any difference *if the Pig had a grandfather called TRESPASSERS WILLIAM*?

He didn't know the answer to any of these questions . . . and he was going to see his first Heffalump in about an hour from now!

Winnie-the-Pooh

I think I am a hundred –
    I'm one.
I'm lying in a forest . . .
    I'm lying in a cave . . .
I'm talking to a Dragon . . .
    I'm BRAVE.

Now We Are Six

"Hallo!" said Tigger, and he sounded so close suddenly that Piglet would have jumped if Pooh hadn't accidentally been sitting on most of him.

The House at Pooh Corner

"Did I really do all that?" he said at last.

"Well," said Pooh, "in poetry – in a piece of poetry – well, you *did* it, Piglet, because the poetry says you did. And that's how people know."

"Oh!" said Piglet. "Because I – I thought I did blinch a little. Just at first. And it says, 'Did he blinch no no.' That's why."

"You only blinched inside," said Pooh, "and that's the bravest way for a Very Small Animal not to blinch that there is."

Piglet sighed with happiness, and began to think about himself. He was BRAVE. . . .

The House at Pooh Corner

MORE FRIENDLY
WITH TWO

In which we find Quotations about Friends and some Relations (mostly Rabbit's)

At first as they stumped along the path which edged the Hundred Acre Wood, they didn't say much to each other; but when they came to the stream, and had helped each other across the stepping stones, and were able to walk side by side again over the heather, they began to talk in a friendly way about this and that, and Piglet said, "If you see what I mean, Pooh," and Pooh said, "It's just what I think myself, Piglet," and Piglet said, "But, on the other hand, Pooh, we must remember," and Pooh said, "Quite true, Piglet, although I had forgotten it for the moment."

Winnie-the-Pooh

"Eeyore," he said solemly, "I, Winnie-the-Pooh, will find your tail for you."

"Thank you, Pooh," answered Eeyore. "You're a real friend," said he. "Not Like Some," he said.

Winnie-the-Pooh

Binker – what I call him – is a
   secret of my own,
And Binker is the reason why I
   never feel alone.
Playing in the nursery, sitting on
   the stair,
Whatever I am busy at, Binker will
   be there.

Now We are Six

"There's a good Tigger. You're just in time for your Strengthening Medicine," and she poured it out for him. Roo said proudly, "I've *had* mine," and Tigger swallowed his and said, "So have I," and then he and Roo pushed each other about in a friendly way, and Tigger accidentally knocked over one or two chairs by accident, and Roo accidently knocked over one on purpose.

The House at Pooh Corner

And then he gave a very long sigh and said, "I wish Pooh were here. It's so much more friendly with two."

Winnie-the-Pooh

"Yes, Christopher Robin?" said Pooh helpfully.

"Pooh, when I'm – *you* know – when I'm *not* doing Nothing, will you come up here sometimes?"

"Just Me?"

"Yes, Pooh."

"Will you be here too?"

"Yes, Pooh, I will be really. I *promise* I will be, Pooh."

"That's good," said Pooh.

The House at Pooh Corner

He trotted along happily, and by-and-by he crossed the stream and came to the place where his friends-and-relations lived. There seemed to be even more of them about than usual this morning, and having nodded to a hedgehog or two, with whom he was too busy to shake hands, and having said, "Good morning, good morning," importantly to some of the others, and "Ah, there you are," kindly, to the smaller ones, he waved a paw at them over his shoulder, and was gone; leaving such an air of excitement and I-don't-know-what behind him, that several members of the Beetle family, including Henry Rush, made their way at once to the Hundred Acre Wood and began climbing trees, in the hope of getting to the top before it happened, whatever it was, so that they might see it properly.

The House at Pooh Corner

Wherever I am, there's always
  Pooh,
There's always Pooh and Me.
Whatever I do, he wants to do.
"Where are you going to-day?" says
  Pooh:

"Well, that's very odd 'cos I was
  too.
Let's go together," says Pooh, says
  he.
"Let's go together," says Pooh.

Now We Are Six

In a little while they were all ready at the top of the Forest, and the Expotition started. First came Christopher Robin and Rabbit, then Piglet and Pooh; then Kanga, with Roo in her pocket, and Owl; then Eeyore; and, at the end, in a long line, all Rabbit's friends-and-relations.

"I didn't ask them," explained Rabbit carelessly. "They just came. They always do. They can march at the end, after Eeyore."

Winnie-the-Pooh

"What I came to say was: Have you seen Small anywhere about?"

"I don't think so," said Pooh. And then, after thinking a little more, he said: "Who is Small?"

"One of my friends-and-relations," said Rabbit carelessly.

This didn't help Pooh much, because Rabbit had so many friends-and-relations, and of such different sorts and sizes, that he didn't know whether he ought to be looking for Small at the top of an oak-tree or in the petal of a buttercup.

"I haven't seen anybody to-day," said Pooh, "not so as to say 'Hallo, Small!' to. Did you want him for anything?"

"*I* don't *want* him," said Rabbit. "But it's always useful to know where a friend-or-relation *is*, whether you want him or whether you don't."

The House at Pooh Corner

"Aha!" said Pooh. (*Rum-tum-tiddle-um-tum*.) "If I know anything about anything, that hole means Rabbit," he said, "and Rabbit means Company," he said, "and Company means Food and Listening-to-Me-Humming and such like. *Rum-tum-tum-tiddle-um*."

Winnie-the-Pooh

Binker's always talking, 'cos I'm
 teaching him to speak:
He sometimes likes to do it in a
 funny sort of squeak,
And he sometimes likes to do it in
 a hoodling sort of roar . . .
And I have to do it for him 'cos his
 throat is rather sore.

Now We Are Six

"Well, could you very kindly tell me where Rabbit is?"

"He has gone to see his friend Pooh Bear, who is a great friend of his."

"But this *is* Me!" said Bear, very much surprised.

"What sort of Me?"

"Pooh Bear."

"Are you sure?" said Rabbit, still more surprised.

"Quite, quite sure," said Pooh.

"Oh, well, then, come in."

Winnie-the-Pooh

"*Hush!*" said Eeyore in a terrible voice to all Rabbit's friends-and-relations, and "Hush!" they said hastily to each other down the line, until it got to the last one of all. And the last and smallest friend-and-relation was so upset to find that the whole Expotition was saying "Hush!" to *him*, that he buried himself head downwards in a crack in the ground, and stayed

there for two days until the danger was over, and then went home in a great hurry, and lived quietly with his Aunt ever-afterwards.

Winnie-the-Pooh

"Suppose *I* carried *my* family about with me in *my* pocket, how many pockets should I want?"

"Sixteen," said Piglet.

"Seventeen, isn't it?" said Rabbit. "And one more for a handkerchief – that's eighteen. Eighteen pockets in one suit! I haven't time."

There was a long and thoughtful silence ... and then Pooh, who had been frowning very hard for some minutes, said: "*I* make it fifteen."

"What?" said Rabbit.

"Fifteen."

"Fifteen what?"

"Your family."

"What about them?"

Pooh rubbed his nose and said that he thought Rabbit had been talking about his family.

"Did I?" said Rabbit carelessly.

Winnie-the-Pooh

So wherever I am, there's always
   Pooh,
There's always Pooh and Me.
"What would I do?" I said to Pooh,
"If it wasn't for you," and Pooh
   said: "True,
It isn't much fun for One, but Two
Can stick together," says Pooh, says
   he.
"That's how it is," says Pooh.

Now We Are Six

"I might have known," said
Eeyore. "After all, one can't complain. I have my friends. Somebody
spoke to me only yesterday. And
was it last week or the week before
that Rabbit bumped into me and
said 'Bother!' The Social Round.
Always something going on."

Winnie-the-Pooh

Piglet sidled up to Pooh from
behind.

"Pooh!" he whispered.

"Yes, Piglet?"

"Nothing," said Piglet, taking
Pooh's paw. "I just wanted to be
sure of you."

The House at Pooh Corner

A VERY
GOOD IDEA

*In which we find Quotations
about Having Good Ideas
and some Not So Good Ones*

"But, Eeyore," said Pooh in distress, "what can we – I mean, how shall we – do you think if we—"

"Yes," said Eeyore. "One of those would be just the thing. Thank you, Pooh."

The House at Pooh Corner

"I think I shall come down."

"How?" asked you.

Winnie-the-Pooh hadn't thought about this. If he let go of the string, he would fall – *bump* – and he didn't like the idea of that. So he thought for a long time, and then he said:

"Christopher Robin, you must shoot the balloon with your gun. Have you got your gun?"

"Of course I have," you said. "But if I do that, it will spoil the balloon," you said.

"But if you *don't*," said Pooh, "I shall have to let go, and that would spoil *me*."

Winnie-the-Pooh

And for the first ten feet Tigger said happily to himself, "Up we go!"

And for the next ten feet he said:

"I always *said* Tiggers could climb trees."

And for the next ten feet he said:

"Not that it's easy, mind you."

And for the next ten feet he said:

"Of course, there's the coming-down too. Backwards."

And then he said:

"Which will be difficult ..."

"Unless one fell ..."

"When it would be ..."

"EASY."

The House at Pooh Corner

Elizabeth Ann
Had a wonderful plan:
She would run round the world till
    she found a man
Who knew *exactly* how God began.

Now We Are Six

The first thing Pooh did was to go to the cupboard to see if he had quite a small jar of honey left; and he had, so he took it down.

"I'm giving this to Eeyore," he explained, "as a present. What are *you* going to give?"

"Couldn't I give it too?" said Piglet. "From both of us?"

"No," said Pooh. "That would *not* be a good plan."

"All right, then, I'll give him a balloon. I've got one left from my party. I'll go and get it now, shall I?"

"That, Piglet, is a *very* good idea. It is just what Eeyore wants to cheer him up. Nobody can be un-cheered with a balloon."

Winnie-the-Pooh

You tied a piece of string to Piglet, and you flew up to the letter-box, with the other end in your beak, and you pushed it through the wire and brought it down to the floor, and you and Pooh pulled hard at this end, and Piglet went slowly up at the other end. And there you were.

"And there Piglet is," said Owl. "If the string doesn't break."

"Supposing it does?" asked Piglet, really wanting to know.

"Then we try another piece of string."

The House at Pooh Corner

"What are you doing?"

"I'm planting a haycorn, Pooh, so that it can grow up into an oak-tree, and have lots of haycorns just outside the front door instead of having to walk miles and miles, do you see, Pooh?"

"Supposing it doesn't?" said Pooh.

"It will, because Christopher Robin says it will, so that's why I'm planting it."

"Well," said Pooh, "if I plant a honeycomb outside my house, then it will grow up into a beehive."

Piglet wasn't quite sure about this.

"Or a *piece* of a honeycomb," said Pooh, "so as not to waste too much. Only then I might only get a piece of a beehive, and it might be the wrong piece, where the bees were buzzing and not hunnying. Bother."

The House at Pooh Corner

73

"How would it be?" said Pooh slowly, "if, as soon as we're out of sight of this Pit, we try to find it again?"

"What's the good of that?" said Rabbit.

"Well," said Pooh, "we keep looking for Home and not finding it, so I thought that if we looked for this Pit, we'd be sure not to find it, which would be a Good Thing, because then we might find something that we *weren't* looking for, which might be just what we *were* looking for, really."

"I don't see much sense in that," said Rabbit.

"No," said Pooh humbly, "there isn't. But there was *going* to be when I began it. It's just that something happened to it on the way."

The House at Pooh Corner

"*I* thought," said Piglet earnestly, "that if Eeyore stood at the bottom of the tree, and if Pooh stood on Eeyore's back, and if I stood on Pooh's shoulders—"

"And if Eeyore's back snapped suddenly, then we could all laugh. Ha ha! Amusing in a quiet way," said Eeyore, "but not really helpful."

"Well," said Piglet meekly, "*I* thought—"

"Would it break your back, Eeyore?" asked Pooh, very much surprised.

"That's what would be so interesting, Pooh. Not being quite sure till afterwards."

The House at Pooh Corner

"It's a Useful Pot," said Pooh. "Here it is. And it's got 'A Very Happy Birthday with love from Pooh' written on it. That's what all that writing is. And it's for putting things in. There!"

When Eeyore saw the pot, he became quite excited.

"Why!" he said. "I believe my Balloon will just go into that Pot!"

"Oh, no, Eeyore," said Pooh. "Balloons are much too big to go into Pots. What you do with a balloon is, you hold the balloon—"

"Not mine," said Eeyore proudly.

Winnie-the-Pooh

"I've got a sort of idea," said Pooh at last, "but I don't suppose it's a very good one."

"I don't suppose it is either," said Eeyore.

"Go on, Pooh," said Rabbit. "Let's have it."

"Well, if we all threw stones and things into the river on *one* side of Eeyore, the stones would make waves, and the waves would wash him to the other side."

"That's a very good idea," said Rabbit, and Pooh looked happy again.

"Very," said Eeyore. "When I want to be washed, Pooh, I'll let you know."

The House at Pooh Corner

74

"Tigger's getting so Bouncy nowadays that it's time we taught him a lesson. Don't you think so, Piglet?"

Piglet said that Tigger *was* very Bouncy, and that if they could think of a way of unbouncing him it would be a Very Good Idea.

The House at Pooh Corner

"I've got an idea!" cried Christopher Robin suddenly.

"Listen to this, Piglet," said Eeyore, "and then you'll know what we're trying to do."

"I'll take off my tunic and we'll each hold a corner, and then Roo and Tigger can jump into it, and it will be all soft and bouncy for them, and they won't hurt themselves."

"*Getting Tigger down*," said Eeyore, "and *Not hurting anybody*. Keep those two ideas in your head, Piglet, and you'll be all right."

The House at Pooh Corner

It was an anxious moment for the watchers on the bridge. They looked and looked . . .

And then, just as Pooh was beginning to think that he must have chosen the wrong stone or the wrong river or the wrong day for his Idea, something grey showed for a moment by the river bank . . . and it got slowly bigger and bigger . . . and at last it was Eeyore coming out.

The House at Pooh Corner

"Well done, Pooh," said Rabbit kindly. "That was a good idea of ours."

"What was?" asked Eeyore.

"Hooshing you to the bank like that."

"*Hooshing* me?" said Eeyore in surprise. "Hooshing *me*? You didn't think I was *hooshed*, did you? I dived. Pooh dropped a large stone on me, and so as not to be struck heavily on the chest, I dived and swam to the bank."

"You didn't really," whispered Piglet to Pooh, so as to comfort him.

"I didn't *think* I did," said Pooh anxiously.

"It's just Eeyore," said Piglet. "*I* thought your Idea was a very good Idea."

The House at Pooh Corner

Then he had an idea, and I think that for a Bear of Very Little Brain, it was a good idea. He said to himself:

"If a bottle can float, then a jar can float, and if a jar floats, I can sit on the top of it, if it's a very big jar."

So he took his biggest jar, and corked it up.

Winnie-the-Pooh

HOW TO WIN
AT POOHSTICKS

In which we find Quotations about Games, Pastimes and Exercises

I'm fishing.
Don't talk, anybody, don't come
    near!
Can't you see that the fish might
    hear?
He thinks I'm playing with a piece
    of string;
He thinks I'm another sort of funny
    sort of thing,
    But he doesn't know I'm fishing –
    He doesn't know I'm fishing.
        That's what I'm doing –
        Fishing.

Now We Are Six

"That's funny," said Pooh. "I dropped it on the other side," said Pooh, "and it came out on this side! I wonder if it would do it again?" And he went back for some more fir-cones.

It did. It kept on doing it. Then he dropped two in at once, and leant over the bridge to see which of them would come out first; and one of them did; but as they were both the same size, he didn't know if it was the one which he wanted to win, or the other one. So the next time he dropped one big one and one little one, and the big one came out first, which was what he had said it would do, and the little one came out last, which was what he said it would do, so he had won twice . . . and when he went home for tea, he had won thirty-six and lost twenty-eight, which meant that he was – that he had – well, you take twenty-eight from thirty-six, and *that's* what he was. Instead of the other way round.

And that was the beginning of the game called Poohsticks, which Pooh invented, and which he and his friends used to play on the edge of the Forest. But they played with sticks instead of fir-cones, because they were easier to mark.

The House at Pooh Corner

"*I* think we all ought to play Poohsticks."

So they did. And Eeyore, who had never played it before, won more times than anybody else; and Roo fell in twice, the first time by accident and the second time on purpose, because he suddenly saw Kanga coming from the Forest, and he knew he'd have to go to bed anyhow. So then Rabbit said he'd go with them; and Tigger and Eeyore went off together, because Eeyore wanted to tell Tigger How to Win at Poohsticks, which you do by letting your stick drop in a twitchy sort of way, if you understand what I mean, Tigger . . .

The House at Pooh Corner

77

He had made up a little hum that very morning, as he was doing his Stoutness Exercises in front of the glass: *Tra-la-la, tra-la-la*, as he stretched up as high as he could go, and then *Tra-la-la, tra-la – oh, help! – la*, as he tried to reach his toes.

Winnie-the-Pooh

Now one day Pooh and Piglet and Rabbit and Roo were all playing Poohsticks together. They had dropped their sticks in when Rabbit said "Go!" and then they had hurried across to the other side of the bridge, and now they were all leaning over the edge, waiting to see whose stick would come out first.

"I can see mine!" cried Roo. "No, I can't, it's something else. Can you see yours, Piglet? I thought I could see mine, but I couldn't. There it is! No, it isn't. Can you see yours, Pooh?"

"No," said Pooh.

"I expect my stick's stuck," said Roo. "Rabbit , my stick's stuck. Is your stick stuck, Piglet?"

"They always take longer than you think," said Rabbit.

"How long do you *think* they'll take?" asked Roo.

The House at Pooh Corner

"He's going *round* and *round*," said Roo, much impressed.

"And why not?" said Eeyore coldly.

"I can swim too," said Roo proudly.

"Not round and round," said Eeyore. "It's much more difficult. I didn't want to come swimming at all to-day," he went on, revolving slowly. "But if, when in, I decide to practice a slight circular movement from right to left – or perhaps I should say," he added, as he got into another eddy, "from left to right, just as it happens to occur to me, it is nobody's business but my own."

The House at Pooh Corner

Christopher Robin goes
Hoppity, hoppity,

Hoppity, hoppity, hop.
Whenever I tell him
Politely to stop it, he
Says he can't possibly stop.

If he stopped hopping, he couldn't
  go anywhere,
Poor little Christopher
Couldn't go anywhere . . .
That's why he *always* goes
Hoppity, hoppity,
Hoppity,
Hoppity,
Hop.

When We Were Very Young

AHA!

In which we find Quotations about Making Traps and Practising Deceptions

"I shall do it," said Pooh, after waiting a little longer, "by means of a trap. And it must be a Cunning Trap, so you will have to help me, Piglet."

"Pooh," said Piglet, feeling quite happy again now, "I will." And then he said, "How shall we do it?" and Pooh said, "That's just it. How?" And then they sat down together to think it out.

Winnie-the-Pooh

"When you go after honey with a balloon, the great thing is not to let the bees know you're coming. Now, if you have a green balloon, they might think you were only part of the tree, and not notice you, and if you have a blue balloon, they might think you were only part of the sky, and not notice you, and the question is: Which is most likely?"

"Wouldn't they notice *you* underneath the balloon?" you asked.

"They might or they might not," said Winnie-the-Pooh. "You never can tell with bees." He thought for a moment and said: "I shall try to look like a small black cloud. That will deceive them."

"Then you had better have the blue balloon," you said; and so it was decided.

Winnie-the-Pooh

"Well, I've got an idea," said Rabbit, "and here it is. We take Tigger for a long explore, somewhere where he's never been, and we lose him there, and next morning we find him again, and – mark my words – he'll be a different Tigger altogether."

"Why?" said Pooh.

"Because he'll be a Humble Tigger. Because he'll be a Sad Tigger, a Melancholy Tigger, a Small and Sorry Tigger, an Oh-Rabbit-I-*am*-glad-to-see-you Tigger. That's why."

The House at Pooh Corner

Pooh's first idea was that they should dig a Very Deep Pit, and then the Heffalump would come along and fall into the Pit, and—

"Why?" said Piglet.

"Why what?" said Pooh.

"Why would he fall in?"

Pooh rubbed his nose with his paw, and said that the Heffalump might be walking along, humming a little song, and looking up at the sky, wondering if it would rain, and so he wouldn't see the Very Deep Pit until he was half-way down, when it would be too late.

Piglet said that this was a very good Trap, but supposing it were raining already?

Pooh rubbed his nose again, and said that he hadn't thought of that. And then he brightened up, and said that, if it were raining already, the Heffalump would be looking at the sky wondering if it would *clear up*, and so he wouldn't see the Very Deep Pit until he was half-way down . . . When it would be too late.

Piglet said that, now that this point had been explained, he thought it was a Cunning Trap.

Pooh was very proud when he heard this, and he felt that the Heffalump was as good as caught already, but there was just one other thing which had to be thought about, and it was this. *Where should they dig the Very Deep Pit?*

Piglet said that the best place would be somewhere where a Heffalump was, just before he fell into it, only about a foot further on.

"But then he would see us digging it," said Pooh.

"Not if he was looking at the sky."

"He would Suspect," said Pooh, "if he happened to look down." He thought for a long time and then added sadly, "It isn't as easy as I thought. I suppose that's why Heffalumps hardly *ever* get caught."

"That must be it," said Piglet.

Winnie-the-Pooh

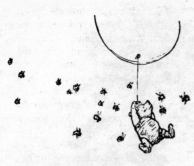

"What do I look like?"

"You look like a Bear holding on to a balloon," you said.

"Not," said Pooh anxiously, " – not like a small black cloud in a blue sky?"

"Not very much."

"Ah, well, perhaps from up here it looks different. And, as I say, you never can tell with bees."

Winnie-the-Pooh

"Have you an umbrella in your house?"

"I think so."

"I wish you would bring it out here, and walk up and down with it, and look up at me every now and then, and say 'Tut-tut, it looks like rain.' I think, if you did that, it would help the deception which we are practising on these bees."

Well, you laughed to yourself, "Silly old Bear!" but you didn't say it aloud because you were so fond of him, and you went home for your umbrella.

Winnie-the-Pooh

"Now listen all of you," said Rabbit when he had finished writing, and Pooh and Piglet sat listening very eagerly with their mouths open. This was what Rabbit read out:

PLAN TO CAPTURE BABY ROO

1. *General Remarks*. Kanga runs faster than any of Us, even Me.
2. *More General Remarks*. Kanga never takes her eye off Baby Roo, except when he's safely buttoned up in her pocket.
3. *Therefore*. If we are to capture Baby Roo, we must get a Long Start, because Kanga runs faster than any of Us, even Me. (*See* 1.)
4. *A Thought*. If Roo had jumped out of Kanga's pocket and Piglet had jumped in, Kanga wouldn't know the difference, because Piglet is a Very Small Animal.
5. Like Roo.
6. But Kanga would have to be looking the other way first, so as not to see Piglet jumping in.
7. See 2.
8. *Another Thought*. But if Pooh was talking to her very excitedly, she *might* look the other way for a moment.
9. And then I could run away with Roo.
10. Quickly.
11. *And Kanga wouldn't discover the difference the until Afterwards*.

Winnie-the-Pooh

81

"The question is, What are we to do about Kanga?"

"Oh, I see," said Pooh.

"The best way," said Rabbit, "would be this. The best way would be to steal Baby Roo and hide him, and then when Kanga says, 'Where's Baby Roo?' we say, '*Aha!*'"

"*Aha!*" said Pooh, practising. "*Aha! Aha!* . . . Of course," he went on, "we could say 'Aha!' even if we hadn't stolen Baby Roo."

"We say '*Aha!*' so that Kanga knows that *we* know where Baby Roo is. '*Aha!*' means 'We'll tell you where Baby Roo is, if you promise to go away from the Forest and never come back.' Now don't talk while I think."

Pooh went into a corner and tried saying 'Aha!' in that sort of voice. Sometimes it seemed to him that it did mean what Rabbit said, and sometimes it seemed to him that it didn't. "I suppose it's just practice," he thought. "I wonder if Kanga will have to practise too so as to understand it."

Winnie-the-Pooh

82

"This is Terrible," thought Piglet. "First he talks in Pooh's voice, and then he talks in Christopher Robin's voice, and he's doing it so as to Unsettle me." And being now Completely Unsettled, he said very quickly and squeakily: "This is a trap for Poohs, and I'm waiting to fall in it, ho-*ho*, what's all this, and then I say ho-*ho* again."

"*What?*" said Christopher Robin.

"A trap for ho-ho's," said Piglet huskily. "I've just made it, and I'm waiting for the ho-ho to come-come."

The House at Pooh Corner

"And – Afterwards?"

"How do you mean?"

"When Kanga *does* Discover the Difference?"

"Then we all say '*Aha!*'"

"All three of us?"

"Yes."

"Oh!"

"Why, what's the trouble, Piglet?"

"Nothing," said Piglet, "as long as *we all three* say it. As long as we all three say it," said Piglet, "I don't mind," he said, "but I shouldn't care to say '*Aha!*' by myself. It wouldn't sound *nearly* so well. By the way," he said, "you *are* quite sure about what you said about the winter months?"

"The winter months?"

"Yes, only being Fierce in the Winter Months."

"Oh, yes, yes, that's all right."

Winnie-the-Pooh

"What's happened?" said Pooh. "Where are we?"

"I think we're in a sort of Pit. I was walking along, looking for somebody, and then suddenly I wasn't any more, and just when I got up to see where I was, something fell on me. And it was you."

"So it was," said Pooh.

"Yes," said Piglet. "Pooh," he went on nervously, and came a little closer, "do you think we're in a Trap?"

Pooh hadn't thought about it at all, but now he nodded. For suddenly he remembered how he and Piglet had once made a Pooh Trap for Heffalumps, and he guessed what had happened. He and Piglet had fallen into a Heffalump Trap for Poohs! That was what it was.

The House at Pooh Corner

83

"Oh, there you are!" called down Winnie-the-Pooh, as soon as you got back to the trees. "I was beginning to get anxious. I have discovered that the bees are now definitely Suspicious."

"Shall I put my umbrella up?" you said.

"Yes, but wait a moment. We must be practical. The important bee to deceive is the Queen Bee. Can you see which is the Queen Bee from down there?"

"No."

"A pity. Well, now, if you walk up and down with your umbrella, saying, 'Tut-tut, it looks like rain,' I shall do what I can by singing a little Cloud Song, such as a cloud might sing . . . Go!"

So, while you walked up and down and wondered if it would rain, Winnie-the-Pooh sang this song:

> How sweet to be a Cloud
>   Floating in the Blue!
> Every little cloud
> *Always* sings aloud.
>
> "How sweet to be a Cloud
>   Floating in the Blue!"
> It makes him very proud
> To be a little cloud.

Winnie-the-Pooh

"*Aha!*" said Piglet, as well as he could after his Terrifying Journey. But it wasn't a very good "*Aha!*" and Kanga didn't seem to understand what it meant.

"Bath first," said Kanga in a cheerful voice.

"*Aha!*" said Piglet again, looking round anxiously for the others. But the others weren't there.

Winnie-the-Pooh

WHAT IS LEARNING?

In which we find Quotations about Reading, Writing, Spelling and Twy-stymes

Piglet comes in for a good many things which Pooh misses; because you can't take Pooh to school without everybody knowing it, but Piglet is so small that he slips into a pocket, where it is very comforting to feel him when you are not quite sure whether twice seven is twelve or twenty-two. Sometimes he slips out and has a good look in the ink-pot, and in this way he has got more education than Pooh, but Pooh doesn't mind. Some have brains, and some haven't, he says, and there it is.

Winnie-the-Pooh

When we asked Pooh what the opposite of an Introduction was, he said "The what of a what?" which didn't help us as much as we had hoped, but luckily Owl kept his head and told us that the Opposite of an Introduction, my dear Pooh, was a Contradiction; and, as he is very good at long words, I am sure that that's what it is.

The House at Pooh Corner

"What's twice eleven?" I said to
   Pooh,
("Twice what?" said Pooh to Me.)
"I *think* it ought to be twenty-two."
"Just what I think myself," said
   Pooh.
"It wasn't an easy sum to do,
But that's what it is," said Pooh,
   said he.
"That's what it is," said Pooh.

Now We Are Six

Eeyore had three sticks on the ground, and was looking at them. Two of the sticks were touching at one end, but not at the other, and the third stick was laid across them. Piglet thought that perhaps it was a Trap of some kind.

"Oh, Eeyore," he began again, "I just—"

"Is that little Piglet?" said Eeyore, still looking hard at his sticks.

"Yes, Eeyore, and I—"

"Do you know what this is?"

"No," said Piglet.

"It's an A."

"Oh," said Piglet.

"Not O – A," said Eeyore severely. "Can't you *hear*, or do you think you have more education than Christopher Robin?"

The House at Pooh Corner

Eight eights are sixty-four,
    Multiply by seven.
When it's done,
Carry one
    And take away eleven.
Nine nines are eighty-one
    Multiply by three.
If it's more,
Carry four,
    And then it's time for tea.

Now We Are Six

"There's a thing called Twystymes," he said.

"Christopher Robin tried to teach it to me once, but it didn't."

"What didn't?" said Rabbit.

"Didn't what?" said Piglet.

Pooh shook his head.

"I don't know," he said. "It just didn't. What are we talking about?"

The House at Pooh Corner

But Owl went on and on, using longer and longer words, until at last he came back to where he started.

Winnie-the-Pooh

Christopher Robin gave me a mastershalum seed, and I planted it, and I'm going to have mastershalums all over the front door."

"I thought they were called nasturtiums," said Piglet timidly, as he went on jumping.

"No," said Pooh. "Not these. These are called mastershalums."

The House at Pooh Corner

"Do you know what A means, little Piglet?"

"No, Eeyore, I don't."

"It means Learning, it means Education, it means all the things that you and Pooh haven't got. That's what A means."

"Oh," said Piglet again. "I mean, does it?" he explained quickly.

"I'm telling you. People come and go in this Forest, and they say, 'It's only Eeyore, so it doesn't count.' They walk to and fro saying 'Ha ha!' But do they know anything about A? They don't. It's just three sticks to *them*. But to the Educated – mark this, little Piglet – to the Educated, not meaning Poohs and Piglets, it's a great and glorious A. Not," he added, "just something that anybody can come and *breathe* on."

The House at Pooh Corner

Suddenly Christopher Robin began to tell Pooh about some of the things: People called Kings and Queens and something called Factors, and a place called Europe, and an island in the middle of the sea where no ships came, and how you make a Suction Pump (if you want to), and when Knights were Knighted, and what comes from Brazil. And Pooh, his back against one of the sixty-something trees, and his paws folded in front of him, said "Oh!" and "I don't know," and thought how wonderful it would be to have a Real Brain which could tell you things.

The House at Pooh Corner

Owl took Christopher Robin's notice from Rabbit and looked at it nervously. He could spell his own name WOL, and he could spell Tuesday so that you knew it wasn't Wednesday, and he could read quite comfortably when you weren't looking over his shoulder and saying "Well?" all the time, and he could –

"Well?" said Rabbit.

"Yes," said Owl, looking Wise and Thoughtful. "I see what you mean. Undoubtedly."

The House at Pooh Corner

"You ought to write '*A Happy Birthday*' on it."

"*That* was what I wanted to ask you," said Pooh. "Because my spelling is Wobbly. It's good spelling but it Wobbles, and the letters get in the wrong places. Would *you* write 'A Happy Birthday' on it for me?"

Winnie-the-Pooh

Owl, wise though he was in many ways, able to read and write and spell his own name WOL, yet somehow went all to pieces over delicate words like MEASLES and BUTTEREDTOAST.

Winnie-the-Pooh

Owl licked the end of his pencil, and wondered how to spell "birthday."

Winnie-the-Pooh

So Owl wrote ... and this is what he wrote:

HIPY PAPY BTHUTHDTH THUTHDA BTHUTHDY.

Pooh looked on admiringly.
"I'm just saying 'A Happy Birthday'," said Owl carelessly.
"It's a nice long one," said Pooh, very much impressed by it.
"Well, *actually*, of course, I'm saying 'A Very Happy Birthday with love from Pooh.' Naturally it takes a good deal of pencil to say a long thing like that."
"Oh, I see," said Pooh.

Winnie-the-Pooh

"Can you read, Pooh?" he asked a little anxiously.
"There's a notice about knocking and ringing outside my door, which Christopher Robin wrote. Could you read it?"
"Christopher Robin told me what it said, and *then* I could."

Winnie-the-Pooh

When Pooh saw what it was, he nearly fell down, he was so pleased. It was a Special Pencil Case. There were pencils in it marked "B" for Bear, and pencils marked "HB" for Helpful Bear, and pencils marked "BB" for Brave Bear. There was a knife for sharpening the pencils, and indiarubber for rubbing out anything which you had spelt wrong, and a ruler for ruling lines for the words to walk on, and inches marked on the ruler in case you wanted to know how many inches anything was, and Blue Pencils and Red Pencils and Green Pencils for saying special things in blue and red and green. And all these lovely things were in little pockets of their own in a Special Case which shut with a click when you clicked it. And they were all for Pooh.

Winnie-the-Pooh

Eeyore was saying to himself. "This writing business. Pencils and what-not. Over-rated, if you ask me. Silly stuff. Nothing in it."

Winnie-the-Pooh

CANDLES AND
PINK SUGAR

*In which we find Quotations
about Birthdays, Parties
and Balloons*

"You seem so sad, Eeyore."

"Sad? Why should I be sad? It's my birthday. The happiest day of the year."

"Your birthday?" said Pooh in great surprise.

"Of course it is. Can't you see? Look at all the presents I have had." He waved a foot from side to side. "Look at the birthday cake. Candles and pink sugar."

Pooh looked – first to the right and then to the left.

"Presents?" said Pooh. "Birthday cake?" said Pooh. "*Where?*"

"Can't you see them?"

"No," said Pooh.

"Neither can I," said Eeyore. "Joke," he explained. "Ha ha!"

Winnie-the-Pooh

"*Bother!*" said Pooh. "What *shall* I do? I *must* give him *something.*"

For a little while he couldn't think of anything. Then he thought: "Well, it's a very nice pot, even if there's no honey in it, and if I washed it clean, and got somebody to write '*A Happy Birthday*' on it, Eeyore could keep things in it, which might be Useful."

Winnie-the-Pooh

"Many happy returns of Eeyore's birthday," said Pooh.

"Oh, is that what it is?"

"What are you giving him, Owl?"

"What are *you* giving him, Pooh?"

"I'm giving him a Useful Pot to Keep Things In, and I wanted to ask you—"

"Is this it?" said Owl, taking it out of Pooh's paw.

"Yes, and I wanted to ask you—"

"Somebody has been keeping honey in it," said Owl.

Winnie-the-Pooh

"Many happy returns of the day," said Piglet again.

"Meaning me?"

"Of course, Eeyore."

"My birthday?"

"Yes."

"Me having a real birthday?"

"Yes, Eeyore, and I've brought you a present."

"Meaning me again?"

"Yes."

"My birthday still?"

"Of course, Eeyore."

"Me going on having a real birthday?"

"Yes, Eeyore, and I brought you a balloon."

"*Balloon?*" said Eeyore. "You did say balloon? One of those big coloured things you blow up? Gaiety, song-and-dance, here we are and there we are?"

Winnie-the-Pooh

"But is it really your birthday?" he asked.

"It is."

"Oh! Well, many happy returns of the day, Eeyore."

"And many happy returns to you, Pooh Bear."

"But it isn't *my* birthday."

"No, it's mine."

"But you said 'Many happy returns'—"

"Well, why not? You don't always want to be miserable on my birthday, do you?"

"Oh, I see," said Pooh.

"It's bad enough," said Eeyore, almost breaking down, "being miserable myself, what with no presents and no cake and no candles, and no proper notice taken of me at all, but if everybody else is going to be miserable too—"

Winnie-the-Pooh

"I wonder if you've got such a thing as a balloon about you?"

"A balloon?"

"Yes, I just said to myself coming along: 'I wonder if Christopher Robin has such a thing as a balloon about him?' I just said it to myself, thinking of balloons, and wondering."

Well, it just happened that you had been to a party the day before at the house of your friend Piglet, and you had balloons at the party. You had had a big green balloon; and one of Rabbit's relations had had a big blue one, and had left it behind, being really too young to go to a party at all; and so you had brought the green one *and* the blue one home with you.

Winnie-the-Pooh

"And didn't *I* give him anything?" asked Christopher Robin sadly.

"Of course you did," I said. "You gave him – don't you remember – a little – a little—"

"I gave him a box of paints to paint things with."

"That was it."

"Why didn't I give it to him in the morning?"

"You were so busy getting his party ready for him. He had a cake with icing on the top, and three candles, and his name in pink sugar, and—"

"Yes, *I* remember," said Christopher Robin.

Winnie-the-Pooh

Eeyore led the way to the most thistly-looking patch of thistles that ever was, and waved a hoof at it.

"A little patch I was keeping for my birthday," he said; "but, after all, what *are* birthdays? Here to-day and gone to-morrow. Help yourself, Tigger."

The House at Pooh Corner

"Many happy returns of the day," called out Pooh, forgetting that he had said it already.

"Thank you, Pooh, I'm having them," said Eeyore gloomily.

Winnie-the-Pooh

"This party," said Christopher Robin, "is a party because of what someone did, and we all know who it was, and it's his party, because of what he did.

Winnie-the-Pooh

91

SOMETHING
OO OCCURRED

In which we find Quotations about Different Kinds of Accident

Eeyore whispered back: "I'm not saying there won't be an Accident *now*, mind you. They're funny things, Accidents. You never have them till you're having them."

The House at Pooh Corner

The next moment the day became very bothering indeed, because Pooh was so busy not looking where he was going that he stepped on a piece of the Forest which had been left out by mistake; and he only just had time to think to himself: "I'm flying. What Owl does. I wonder how you stop – " when he stopped.

Bump!

Winnie-the-Pooh

"Ah, Piglet," said Owl, looking very much annoyed; "where's Pooh?"

"I'm not quite sure," said Pooh.

The House at Pooh Corner

"But who did it?" asked Roo. Eeyore didn't answer.

"I expect it was Tigger," said Piglet nervously.

"But, Eeyore," said Pooh, "was it a Joke, or an Accident? I mean—"

"I didn't stop to ask, Pooh. Even at the very bottom of the river I didn't stop to say to myself, '*Is* this a Hearty Joke or is it the Merest Accident?' I just floated to the surface, and said to myself, 'It's wet.' If you know what I mean."

The House at Pooh Corner

"H–hup!" said Roo accidentally.

"Roo, dear!" said Kanga reproachfully.

"Was it me?" asked Roo, a little surprised.

Winnie-the-Pooh

Kanga was jumping along the bank, saying "Are you *sure* you're all right, Roo dear?" to which Roo, from whatever pool he was in at the moment, was answering "Look at me swimming!" Eeyore had turned round and hung his tail over the first pool into which Roo fell, and with his back to the accident was grumbling quietly to himself, and saying, "All this washing; but catch on to my tail, little Roo, and you'll be all right."

Winnie-the-Pooh

"Ow!" squeaked something. "That's funny," thought Pooh. "I said 'Ow!' without really oo'ing."

"Help!" said a small, high voice.

"That's me again," thought Pooh. "I've had an Accident, and fallen down a well, and my voice has gone all squeaky and works before I'm ready for it, because I've done something to myself inside. Bother!"

The House at Pooh Corner

"Well, that's funny," he thought. "I wonder what that bang was. I couldn't have made such a noise just falling down. And where's my balloon? And what's that small piece of damp rag doing?"

It was the balloon!

"Oh, dear!" said Piglet. "Oh, dear, oh, dearie, dearie, dear! Well, it's too late now. I can't go back, and I haven't another balloon, and perhaps Eeyore doesn't *like* balloons so *very* much."

Winnie-the-Pooh

"Oh!" said Piglet. "Well, did Owl *always* have a letter-box in his ceiling?"

"Has he?"

"Yes, look."

"I can't," said Pooh. "I'm face downwards under something, and that, Piglet, is a very bad position for looking at ceilings."

"Well, he has, Pooh."

"Perhaps he's changed it," said Pooh. "Just for a change."

The House at Pooh Corner

Bear began to sigh, and then found he couldn't because he was so tightly stuck; and a tear rolled down his eye, as he said:

"Then would you read a Sustaining Book, such as would help and comfort a Wedged Bear in Great Tightness?"

Winnie-the-Pooh

"Yes, but I'm afraid – I'm very sorry, Eeyore – but when I was running along to bring it to you, I fell down."

"Dear, dear, how unlucky! You ran too fast, I expect. You didn't hurt yourself, Little Piglet?"

"No, but I – I – oh, Eeyore, I burst the balloon!"

There was a very long silence.

"My balloon?" said Eeyore at last.

Piglet nodded.

"My birthday balloon?"

"Yes, Eeyore," said Piglet, sniffing a little. "Here it is. With – with many happy returns of the day." And he gave Eeyore the small piece of damp rag.

"Is this it?" said Eeyore, a little surprised.

Piglet nodded.

"My present?"

Piglet nodded again.

"The balloon?"

"Yes."

"Thank you, Piglet," said Eeyore.

Winnie-the-Pooh

Thus, nose to pane, he pondered;
but
The lattice window, loosely shut,
Swung open. With one startled
  "Oh!"
Our Teddy disappeared below.

There happened to be passing by
A plump man with a twinkling eye,
Who, seeing Teddy in the street,
Raised him politely to his feet,
And murmured kindly in his ear
Soft words of comfort and of cheer:
"Well, well!" "Allow me!" "Not at
  all."
"Tut-tut! A very nasty fall."

When We Were Very Young

"I ought to say," explained Pooh as they walked down to the shore of the island, "that it isn't just an ordinary sort of boat. Sometimes it's a Boat, and sometimes it's more of an Accident. It all depends."

"Depends on what?"

"On whether I'm on the top of it or underneath it."

Winnie-the-Pooh

Here lies a tree which Owl (a bird)
  Was fond of when it stood on
  end,
  And Owl was talking to a friend
Called Me (in case you hadn't
  heard)
When something Oo occurred.

The House at Pooh Corner

"Supposing we hit him by mistake?" said Piglet anxiously.

"Or supposing you missed him by mistake," said Eeyore. "Think of all the possibilities, Piglet, before you settle down to enjoy yourselves."

The House at Pooh Corner

"Or suppose I get stuck in his front door again, coming out, as I did once when his front door wasn't big enough?"

"Because I *know* I'm not getting fatter, but his front door may be getting thinner."

The House at Pooh Corner

"Oh!" said Pooh, and scrambled up as quickly as he could. "Did I fall on you, Piglet?"

"You fell on me," said Piglet, feeling himself all over.

"I didn't mean to," said Pooh sorrowfully.

"I didn't mean to be underneath," said Piglet sadly. "But I'm all right now, Pooh, and I *am* so glad it was you."

The House at Pooh Corner

Piglet still felt that to be underneath a Very Good Dropper would be a Mistake, and he was just going to hurry back for something which he had forgotten when the Jagular called out to them.

"Help! Help!" it called.

"That's what Jagulars always do," said Pooh, much interested. "They call 'Help! Help!' and then when you look up, they drop on you."

"I'm looking *down*," cried Piglet loudly, so as the Jagular shouldn't do the wrong thing by accident.

The House at Pooh Corner

"*Ow!*" said Tigger.

He sat down and put his paw in his mouth.

"What's the matter?" asked Pooh.

"*Hot!*" mumbled Tigger.

"Your friend," said Eeyore, "appears to have bitten on a bee."

The House at Pooh Corner

"Somebody BOUNCED me. I was just thinking by the side of the river – thinking, if any of you know what that means – when I received a loud BOUNCE."

"Oh, Eeyore!" said everybody.

"Are you sure you didn't slip?" asked Rabbit wisely.

"Of course I slipped. If you're standing on the slippery bank of a river, and somebody BOUNCES you loudly from behind, you slip. What did you think I did?"

The House at Pooh Corner

"*Ow!*" said Pooh.

"Did I miss?" you asked.

"You didn't exactly *miss*," said Pooh, "but you missed the *balloon*."

Winnie-the-Pooh

A MYSTERIOUS MISSAGE

*In which we find Quotations
about Notices, Messages
and Rissolutions*

"Yesterday morning," said Rabbit solemnly, "I went to see Christopher Robin. He was out. Pinned on his door was a notice!"

"The same notice?"

"A different one. But the meaning was the same. It's very odd."

"Amazing," said Owl, looking at the notice again, and getting, just for a moment, a curious sort of feeling that something had happened to Christopher Robin's back. "What did you do?"

"Nothing."

"The best thing," said Owl wisely.

The House at Pooh Corner

Pooh had had a Mysterious Missage underneath his front door that morning, saying, "**I AM SCERCHING FOR A NEW HOUSE FOR OWL SO HAD YOU RABBIT,**" and while he was wondering what it meant Rabbit had come in and read it for him.

"I'm leaving one for all the others," said Rabbit, "and telling them what it means, and they'll all search too. I'm in a hurry, goodbye." And he had run off.

The House at Pooh Corner

"I had a Very Important Missage sent me in a bottle, and owing to having got some water in my eyes, I couldn't read it, so I brought it to you.

Winnie-the-Pooh

Underneath the knocker there was a notice which said:

PLES RING IF AN RNSER IS
REQIRD.

Underneath the bell-pull there was a notice which said:

PLEZ CNOKE IF AN RNSR IS NOT
REQID.

Winnie-the-Pooh

"Bother!" said Rabbit. "He's gone out."

He went back to the green front door, just to make sure, and he was turning away, feeling that his morning had got all spoilt, when he saw a piece of paper on the ground. And there was a pin in it, as if it had fallen off the door.

"Ha!" said Rabbit, feeling quite happy again. "Another notice!"

This is what it said:

GON OUT
BACKSON
BISY
BACKSON
C.R.

"Ha!" said Rabbit again. "I must tell the others." And he hurried off importantly.

The House at Pooh Corner

"Well?" said Rabbit again, as Owl knew he was going to.

"Exactly," said Owl.

For a little while he couldn't think of anything more; and then, all of a sudden, he had an idea.

"Tell me, Rabbit," he said, "The *exact* words of the first notice. This is very important. Everything depends on this. The *exact* words

of the *first* notice."

"It was just the same as that one really."

Owl looked at him, and wondered whether to push him off the tree; but, feeling that he could always do it afterwards, he tried once more to find out what they were talking about.

The House at Pooh Corner

98

Owl looked at the notice again. To one of his education the reading of it was easy. "Gon out, Backson. Bisy, Backson" – just the sort of thing you'd expect to see on a notice.

"It is quite clear what has happened, my dear Rabbit," he said. "Christopher Robin has gone out somewhere with Backson. He and Backson are busy together. Have you seen a Backson anywhere about in the Forest lately?"

"I don't know," said Rabbit. "That's what I came to ask you. What are they like?"

The House at Pooh Corner

King John
Put up a notice,
"LOST or STOLEN or
    STRAYED!
JAMES JAMES
MORRISON'S MOTHER
SEEMS TO HAVE BEEN
    MISLAID.
LAST SEEN
WANDERING VAGUELY:
QUITE OF HER OWN ACCORD,
SHE TRIED TO GET DOWN
TO THE END OF THE TOWN –
**FORTY SHILLINGS
REWARD!**

When We Were Very Young

They stuck the pole in the ground, and Christopher Robin tied a message on to it:

NorTH PoLE
DICSovERED By
PooH
PooH FouND IT

Then they all went home again.

Winnie-the-Pooh

At last he found a pencil and a small piece of dry paper, and a bottle with a cork to it. And he wrote on one side of the paper:

HELP!
PIGLIT (ME)

and on the other side:

IT'S ME PIGLIT, HELP HELP!

Winnie-the-Pooh

Rabbit brained out a Notice, and this is what it said:

"Notice a meeting of everybody will meet at the House at Pooh Corner to pass a Rissolution By Order Keep to the Left Signed Rabbit."

He had to write this out two or three times before he could get the rissolution to look like what he thought it was going to when he began to spell it; but, when at last it was finished, he took it round to everybody and read it out to them. And they all said they would come.

The House at Pooh Corner

"It's a Missage," he said to himself, "that's what it is. And that letter is a 'P,' and so is that, and so is that, and 'P' means 'Pooh,' so it's a very important Missage to me, and I can't read it. I must find Christopher Robin or Owl or Piglet, one of those Clever Readers who can read things, and they will tell me what this missage means. Only I can't swim. Bother!"

Winnie-the-Pooh

"The rissolution," said Rabbit, "is that we all sign it, and take it to Christopher Robin."

So it was signed PooH, WOL, PIGLET, EOR, RABBIT, KANGA, BLOT, SMUDGE.

The House at Pooh Corner

100

Next morning the notice on Christopher Robin's door said:

GONE OUT
BACK SOON
C. R.

Which is why all the animals in the Forest – except, of course, the Spotted and Herbaceous Backson – now know what Christopher Robin does in the mornings.

The House at Pooh Corner

eOR

"And what about the new house?" asked Pooh. "Have you found it, Owl?"

"He's found a name for it," said Christopher Robin, lazily nibbling at a piece of grass, "so now all he wants is the house."

"I am calling it this," said Owl importantly, and he showed them what he had been making. It was a square piece of board with the name of the house painted on it:

THE WOLERY
The House at Pooh Corner

"We all know why we're here," he said, "but I have asked my friend Eeyore—"

"That's Me," said Eeyore. "Grand."

"I have asked him to Propose a Rissolution." And he sat down again. "Now then, Eeyore," he said.

"Don't Bustle me," said Eeyore, getting up slowly.

"Don't now-then me." He took a piece of paper from behind his ear, and unfolded it. "Nobody knows anything about this," he went on. "This is a Surprise."

The House at Pooh Corner

INTERESTING ANECDOTES

*In which we find Quotations
about Useful Information
(Mainly by Owl)*

"Half an hour," said Owl, settling himself comfortably. "That will just give me time to finish that story I was telling you about my Uncle Robert – a portrait of whom you see underneath you. Now let me see, where was I? Oh, yes. It was on just such a blusterous day as this that my Uncle Robert—"

Pooh closed his eyes.

The House at Pooh Corner

One night it happened that he took
A peep at an old picture-book,
Wherein he came across by chance
The picture of a King of France
(A stoutish man) and, down below,
These words: "King Louis So and So,
Nicknamed 'The Handsome!' "
   There he sat,
And (think of it!) the man was fat!

When We Were Very Young

Owl was telling Kanga an Interesting Anecdote full of long words like Encyclopaedia and Rhododendron to which Kanga wasn't listening.

Winnie-the-Pooh

102

In after-years he liked to think that he had been in Very Great Danger during the Terrible Flood, but the only danger he had really been in was the last half-hour of his imprisonment, when Owl, who had just flown up, sat on a branch of his tree to comfort him, and told him a very long story about an aunt who had once laid a seagull's egg by mistake, and the story went on and on, rather like this sentence, until Piglet who was listening out of his window without much hope, went to sleep quietly and naturally, slipping slowly out of the window towards the water until he was only hanging on by his toes, at which moment, luckily, a sudden loud squawk from Owl, which was really part of the story, being what his aunt said, woke the Piglet up and just gave him time to jerk himself back into safety and say, "How interesting, and did she?"

Winnie-the-Pooh

Owl was explaining that in a case of Sudden and Temporary Immersion the Important Thing was to keep the Head Above Water;

The House at Pooh Corner

"Could you fly up to the letter-box with Piglet on your back?" he asked.

"No," said Piglet quickly. "He couldn't."

Owl explained about the Necessary Dorsal Muscles. He had explained this to Pooh and Christopher Robin once before, and had been waiting ever since for a chance to do it again, because it is a thing which you can easily explain twice before anybody knows what you are talking about.

The House at Pooh Corner

"You don't mind my asking," he went on, "but what colour was this balloon when it – when it *was* a balloon?"

"Red."

"I just wondered ... Red," he murmured to himself. "My favourite colour ... How big was it?"

"About as big as me."

"I just wondered ... About as big as Piglet," he said to himself sadly. "My favourite size. Well, well."

Winnie-the-Pooh

There was a small spinney of larch-trees just here, and it seemed as if the two Woozles, if that is what they were, had been going round this spinney; so round this spinney went Pooh and Piglet after them; Piglet passing the time by telling Pooh what his Grandfather Trespassers W had done to Remove Stiffness after Tracking, and how his Grandfather Trespassers W had suffered in his later years from Shortness of Breath, and other matters of interest, and Pooh wondering what a Grandfather was like, and if perhaps this was Two Grandfathers they were after now, and, if so, whether he would be allowed to take one home and keep it, and what Christopher Robin would say. And still the tracks went on in front of them ...

Winnie-the-Pooh

They're changing guard at
   Buckingham Palace –
Christopher Robin went down with
   Alice.

We saw a guard in a sentry-box.
"One of the sergeants looks after
   their socks,"
           Says Alice.
When We Were Very Young

NOT VERY
HOW

In which we find Quotations about Feeling Terrible, Sad and Pathetic (Chiefly by Eeyore)

"And how are you?" said Winnie-the-Pooh.

Eeyore shook his head from side to side.

"Not very how," he said. "I don't seem to have felt at all how for a long time."

Winnie-the-Pooh

"Why, what's the matter?"

"Nothing, Pooh Bear, nothing. We can't all, and some of us don't. That's all there is to it."

"Can't all *what?*" said Pooh, rubbing his nose.

"Gaiety. Song-and-dance. Here we go round the mulberry bush."

"Oh!" said Pooh. He thought for a long time, and then asked, "What mulberry bush is that?"

"Bon-hommy," went on Eeyore gloomily. "French word meaning bonhommy," he explained. "I'm not complaining, but There It Is."

Winnie-the-Pooh

"That's right," said Eeyore. "Sing. Umty-tiddly, umty-too. Here we go gathering Nuts and May. Enjoy yourself."

"I am," said Pooh.

"Some can," said Eeyore.

Winnie-the-Pooh

"Good morning, Eeyore," shouted Piglet.

"Good morning, Little Piglet," said Eeyore. "If it *is* a good morning," he said. "Which I doubt," said he. "Not that it matters," he said.

Winnie-the-Pooh

"Well, we're very glad to see you, Eeyore, and now we're going on to see owl."

"That's right. You'll like Owl. He flew past a day or two ago and noticed me. He didn't actually say anything, mind you, but he knew it was me. Very friendly of him, I thought. Encouraging."

The House at Pooh Corner

Eeyore, the old grey Donkey, stood by the side of the stream, and looked at himself in the water.

"Pathetic," he said. "That's what it is. Pathetic."

He turned and walked slowly down the stream for twenty yards, splashed across it, and walked slowly back on the other side. Then he looked at himself in the water again.

"As I thought," he said. "No better from *this* side. But nobody minds. Nobody cares. Pathetic, that's what it is."

Winnie-the-Pooh

106

"Well," said Eeyore that afternoon, when he saw them all walking up to his house, "this *is* a surprise. Am *I* asked too?"

The House at Pooh Corner

"I'm not asking anybody," said Eeyore. "I'm just telling everybody. We can look for the North Pole, or we can play 'Here we go gathering Nuts and May' with the end part of an ants' nest. It's all the same to me."

Winnie-the-Pooh

"We're starting," said Rabbit. "I must go." And he hurried off to the front of the Expotition with Christopher Robin.

"All right," said Eeyore. "We're going. Only Don't Blame Me."

Winnie-the-Pooh

"Have you all got something?" asked Christopher Robin with his mouth full.

"All except me," said Eeyore. "As usual." He looked round at them in his melancholy way.

Winnie-the-Pooh

Everybody said "How-do-you-do" to Eeyore, and Eeyore said that he didn't, not to notice, and then they sat down.

The House at Pooh Corner

So Eeyore stood there, gazing sadly at the ground, and Winnie-the-Pooh walked all round him once.

"Why, what's happened to your tail?" he said in surprise.

"What *has* happened to it?" said Eeyore.

"It isn't there!"

"Are you sure?"

"Well, either a tail *is* there or it isn't there. You can't make a mistake about it, and yours *isn't* there!"

"Then what is?"

"Nothing." ...

"That Accounts for a Good Deal," said Eeyore gloomily. "It Explains Everything. No Wonder."

"You must have left it somewhere," said Winnie-the-Pooh.

"Somebody must have taken it," said Eeyore. "How Like Them," he added, after a long silence.

Winnie-the-Pooh

"I don't hold with all the washing," grumbled Eeyor. "This modern Behind-the-ears nonsense."

Winnie the Pooh

"Hallo, Pooh," he said. "How's things?"

"Terrible and Sad," said Pooh, "because Eeyore, who is a friend of mine, has lost his tail. And he's Moping about it.

Winnie-the-Pooh

"Same to you, Pooh Bear, and twice on Thursdays," said Eeyore gloomily. .

The House at Pooh Corner

"Oh, Eeyore, you *are* wet!" said Piglet, feeling him.

Eeyore shook himself, and asked somebody to explain to Piglet what happened when you had been inside a river for quite a long time.

The House at Pooh Corner

"*Could* you ask your friend to do his exercises somewhere else? I shall be having lunch directly, and don't want it bounced on just before I begin. A trifling matter, and fussy of me, but we all have our little ways."

The House at Pooh Corner

And two days later Rabbit happened to meet Eeyore in the Forest.

"Hallo, Eeyore," he said, "what are *you* looking for?"

"Small, of course," said Eeyore. "Haven't you any brain?"

"Oh, but didn't I tell you?" said Rabbit. "Small was found two days ago."

There was a moment's silence.

"Ha-ha," said Eeyore bitterly. "Merriment and what-not. Don't apologize. It's just what *would* happen."

The House at Pooh Corner

Christopher Robin and Pooh and Piglet picked themselves up first, then they picked Tigger up, and underneath everybody else was Eeyore.

"Oh, Eeyore!" cried Christopher Robin. "Are you hurt?" And he felt him rather anxiously, and dusted him and helped him to stand up again.

Eeyore said nothing for a long time. And then he said "Is Tigger there?"

Tigger was there, feeling Bouncy again already.

"Yes," said Christopher Robin. "Tigger's here."

"Well, just thank him for me," said Eeyore.

The House at Pooh Corner

Eeyore took his tail out of the water, and swished it from side to side.

"As I expected," he said. "Lost all feeling. Numbed it. That's what it's done. Numbed it. Well, as long as nobody minds, I suppose it's all right."

Winnie-the-Pooh

"Nobody tells me," said Eeyore. "Nobody keeps me informed. I make it seventeen days come Friday since anybody spoke to me."

"It certainly isn't seventeen days—"

"Come Friday," explained Eeyore.

"And to-day's Saturday," said Rabbit. "So that would make it eleven days. And I was here myself a week ago."

"Not conversing," said Eeyore. "Not first one and then the other. You said 'Hallo' and Flashed Past. I saw your tail a hundred yards up the hill as I was meditating my reply. I *had* thought of saying 'What?' – but of, course, it was then too late."

"Well, I was in a hurry."

"No Give and Take," Eeyore went on. "No Exchange of Thought. '*Hallo - What*'—I mean, it gets you nowhere, particularly if the other person's tail is only just in sight for the second half of the conversation."

The House at Pooh Corner

Eeyore was sitting with his tail in the water when they all got back to him.

"Tell Roo to be quick, some-body," he said. "My tail's getting cold. I don't want to mention it, but I just mention it. I don't want to complain, but there it is. My tail's cold."

Winnie-the-Pooh

"Eeyore," said Owl, "Christopher Robin is giving a party."

"Very interesting," said Eeyore. "I suppose they will be sending me down the odd bits which got trodden on. Kind and Thoughtful. Not at all, don't mention it."

Winnie-the-Pooh

"What I say," said Eeyore, "is that it's unsettling. I didn't want to come to the Expo – what Pooh said. I only came to oblige. But here I am; and I am the end of the Expo – what we're talking about – then let me *be* the end. But if, every time I want to sit down for a little rest, I have to brush away half a dozen of Rabbit's smaller friends-and-relations first, then this isn't an Expo – whatever it is – at all, it's simply a Confused Noise. That's what *I* say."

Winnie-the-Pooh

And all the time Winnie-the-Pooh had been trying to get the honey-jar off his head. The more he shook it, the more tightly it stuck. "*Bother!*" he said, inside the jar, and "*Oh, help!*" and, mostly, "*Ow!*" And he tried bumping it against things, but as he couldn't see what he was bumping it against, it didn't help him; and he tried to climb out of the Trap, but as he could see nothing but jar, and not much of that, he couldn't find his way. So at last he lifted up his head, jar and all, and made a loud, roaring noise of Sadness and Despair . . .

Winnie-the-Pooh

"If anybody wants to clap," said Eeyore when he had read this, "now is the time to do it."

They all clapped.

"Thank you," said Eeyore. "Unexpected and gratifying, if a little lacking in Smack."

The House at Pooh Corner

Piglet explained to Tigger that he mustn't mind what Eeyore said because he was *always* gloomy; and Eeyore explained to Piglet that, on the contrary, he was feeling particularly cheerful this morning.

The House at Pooh Corner

I KNOW YOU KNOW
AND I WISH
YOU'D TELL

In which we find Quotations about Difficult Questions

Elizabeth Ann
Said to her Nan:
"Please will you tell me how God
   began?
Somebody must have made Him. So
Who could it be, 'cos I want to
   know?"
And nurse said, "*Well!*"
And Ann said, "Well?
I know you know, and I wish you'd
   tell."
And nurse took pins from her
   mouth, and said,
"Now then, darling, it's time for
bed."

Now We Are Six

"Did he say Good-bye-and-
thank-you-for-a-nice-time?" said
Rabbit.

"He only just said how-do-you-
do," said Christopher Robin.

"Ha!" said Rabbit. After thinking
a little, he went on: "Has he written
a letter saying how much he enjoyed
himself, and how sorry he was he
had to go so suddenly?"

Christopher Robin didn't think
he had

"Ha!" said Rabbit again, and
looked very important. "This is
Serious. He is Lost. We must begin
the Search at once."

The House at Pooh Corner

"Well?'
"Exactly," said Owl. "Precisely."
And he added, after a little thought,
"If you had not come to me, I
should have come to you."

"Why?" asked Rabbit.

"For that very reason," said Owl,
hoping that something helpful
would happen soon.

The House at Pooh Corner

"Is this it?" said Eeyore, a
little surprised.

Piglet nodded.

"My present?"

Piglet nodded again.

"The balloon?'

"Yes."

"Thank you, Piglet," said Eeyore.

Winnie-the-Pooh

"Hallo, Rabbit," he said, "is that you?"

"Let's pretend it isn't," said Rabbit, "and see what happens."

Winnie-the-Pooh

"Don't *you* know what Tiggers like?" asked Pooh.

"I expect if I thought hard I should," said Christopher Robin, "but I *thought* Tigger knew."

"I do," said Tigger. "Everything there is in the world except honey and haycorns and – what were those hot things called?"

"Thistles."

"Yes, and those."

The House at Pooh Corner

"It's – I wondered – It's only – Rabbit, I suppose *you* don't know. What does the North Pole *look* like?"

"Well," said Rabbit, stroking his whiskers, "Now you're asking me."

"I did know once, only I've sort of forgotten," said Christopher Robin carelessly.

"It's a funny thing," said Rabbit, "but I've sort of forgotten too, although I did know *once*."

"I suppose it's just a pole stuck in the ground?"

"Sure to be a pole," said Rabbit, "because of calling it a pole, and if it's a pole, well, I should think it would be sticking in the ground, shouldn't you, because there'd be nowhere else to stick it."

"Yes, that's what I thought."

"The only thing," said Rabbit, "is *where is it sticking?*"

"That's what we're looking for," said Christopher Robin.

Winnie-the-Pooh

112

Nobody seemed to know where they came from, but there they were in the Forest: Kanga and Baby Roo. When Pooh asked Christopher Robin, "How did they come here?" Christopher Robin said, "In the Usual Way, if you know what I mean, Pooh," and Pooh, who didn't, said "Oh!" Then he nodded his head twice and said, "In the Usual Way. Ah!"

Winnie-the-Pooh

"I didn't know you were playing," said Roo.

"I'm not," said Eeyore.

"Eeyore, what *are* you doing there?" said Rabbit.

"I'll give you three guesses, Rabbit. Digging holes in the ground? Wrong. Leaping from branch to branch of a young oak-tree? Wrong. Waiting for somebody to help me out of the river? Right. Give Rabbit time, and he'll get the answer."

The House at Pooh Corner

"I shall have to go and find them," explained Tigger to Roo.

"May I find them too?" asked Roo eagerly.

"I think not to-day, dear," said Kanga. "Another day."

"Well, if they're lost to-morrow, may I find them?"

"We'll see," said Kanga, and Roo, who knew what *that* meant, went into a corner and practised jumping out at himself, partly because he wanted to practise this, and partly because he didn't want Christopher Robin and Tigger to think that he minded when they went off without him.

The House at Pooh Corner

"I think not to-day, dear. Another day."

"To-morrow?" said Roo hopefully.

"We'll see," said Kanga.

"You're always seeing, and nothing ever happens," said Roo sadly.

The House at Pooh Corner

You remember how he discovered the North Pole; well, he was so proud of this that he asked Christopher Robin if there were any other Poles such as a Bear of Little Brain might discover.

"There's a South Pole," said Christopher Robin, "and I expect there's an East Pole and a West Pole, though people don't like talking about them."

Winnie-the-Pooh

"It's a funny thing about Tiggers," whispered Tigger to Roo, "how Tiggers *never* get lost."

"Why don't they, Tigger?"

"They just don't," explained Tigger. "That's how it is."

The House at Pooh Corner

On Monday, when the sun is hot
I wonder to myself a lot:
"Now is it true, or is it not,
"That what is which and which is
      what?"

On Tuesday, when it hails and
      snows,
The feeling on me grows and grows
That hardly anybody knows
If those are these or these are those.

On Wednesday, when the sky is
      blue,
And I have nothing else to do,
I sometimes wonder if it's true
That who is what and what is who.

On Thursday, when it starts to
      freeze
And hoar-frost twinkles on the
      trees,
How very readily one sees
That these are whose – but whose
      are these?

Winnie-the-Pooh

"What do you like doing best in the world, Pooh?"

"Well," said Pooh, "what I like best—" and then he had to stop and think. Because although Eating Honey *was* a very good thing to do, there was a moment just before you began to eat it which was better than when you were, but he didn't know what it was called. And then he thought that being with Christopher Robin was a very good thing to do, and having Piglet near was a very friendly thing to have; and so, when he had thought it all out, he said, "What I like best in the whole world is Me and Piglet going to see You, and You saying 'What about a little something?' and Me saying, 'Well, I shouldn't mind a little something, should you, Piglet,' and it being a hummy sort of day outside, and birds singing."

The House at Pooh Corner

Slowly and slowly
    Dawns the new day . . .
What's become of John boy?

    No one can say.
Some think that John boy
    Is lost on the hill;
Some say he won't come back,
    Some say he will.

Now We Are Six

114

And as they went, Tigger told Roo (who wanted to know) all about the things that Tiggers could do.

"Can they fly?" asked Roo.

"Yes," said Tigger, "they're very good flyers, Tiggers are. Strornry good flyers."

"Oo!" said Roo. "Can they fly as well as Owl?"

"Yes," said Tigger. "Only they don't want to."

"Why don't they want to?"

"Well, they just don't like it, somehow."

Roo couldn't understand this, because he thought it would be lovely to be able to fly, but Tigger said it was difficult to explain to anybody who wasn't a Tigger himself.

The House at Pooh Corner

"What I like *doing* best is Nothing."

"How do you do Nothing?" asked Pooh, after he had wondered for a long time.

"Well, it's when people call out at you just as you're going off to do it, 'What are you going to do, Christopher Robin?' and you say 'Oh, nothing,' and then you go and do it."

"Oh, I see," said Pooh.

"This is a nothing sort of thing that we're doing now."

"Oh, I see," said Pooh again.

"It means just going along, listening to all the things you can't hear, and not bothering."

"Oh!" said Pooh.

The House at Pooh Corner

"That was a lovely bit just now, when you pretended we were going to fall-bump-to-the-bottom, and we didn't. Will you do that bit again?"

"NO," said Tigger.

The House at Pooh Corner

"I *love* jumping." said Roo. "Let's see who can jump farthest, you or me."

"*I* can," said Tigger. "But we mustn't stop now, or we shall be late."

"Late for what?"

"For whatever we want to be in time for," said Tigger, hurrying on.

The House at Pooh Corner

Elizabeth Ann went home again
And took from the ottoman Jennifer
  Jane.
"Jenniferjane," said Elizabeth Ann,
"Tell me *at once* how God began."
And Jane, who didn't much care
  for speaking,
Replied in her usual way by
  squeaking.

What did it mean? Well, to be quite
  candid,
I don't know, but Elizabeth Ann
  did.
Elizabeth Ann said softly, "O!
Thank you, Jennifer. Now I know."

Now We Are Six

Pooh looked at his two paws. He knew that one of them was the right, and he knew that when you had decided which one of them was the right, then the other one was the left, but he never could remember how to begin.

The House at Pooh Corner

Christopher Robin was going away. Nobody knew why he was going; nobody knew where he was going; indeed, nobody even knew why he knew that Christopher Robin *was* going away. But somehow or other everybody in the Forest felt that it was happening at last. Even Smallest-of-all, a friend-and-relation of Rabbit's who thought he had once seen Christopher Robin's foot, but couldn't be quite sure because perhaps it was something else, even C. of A. told himself that Things were going to be Different; and Late and Early, two other friends-and-relations, said, "Well, Early?" and "Well, Late?" to each other in such a hopeless sort of way that it really didn't seem any good waiting for the answer.

The House at Pooh Corner

"Pooh, *promise* you won't forget about me, ever. Not even when I'm a hundred."

Pooh thought for a little.

"How old shall *I* be then?"

"Ninety-nine."

Pooh nodded.

"I promise," he said.

The House at Pooh Corner

EVERYBODY IS
ALL RIGHT, REALLY

*In which we find Quotations
about Getting On With
(and Putting Up With) Others*

Piglet thought that they ought to have a Reason for going to see everybody, like Looking for Small or Organizing an Expotition, if Pooh could think of something.

Pooh could.

"We'll go because it's Thursday," he said, "and we'll go to wish everybody a Very Happy Thursday. Come on, Piglet."

The House at Pooh Corner

So after breakfast they went round to see Piglet, and Pooh explained as they went that Piglet was a Very Small Animal who didn't like bouncing, and asked Tigger not to be too Bouncy just at first. And Tigger, who had been hiding behind trees and jumping out on Pooh's shadow when it wasn't looking, said that Tiggers were only bouncy before breakfast, and that as soon as they had had a few haycorns they became Quiet and Refined.

The House at Pooh Corner

"It's your fault, Eeyore. You've never been to see any of us. You just stay here in this one corner of the Forest waiting for the others to come to *you*. Why don't you go to *them* sometimes?" Eeyore was silent for a little while, thinking.

"There may be something in what you say, Rabbit," he said at last. "I have been neglecting you. I must move about more. I must come and go."

"That's right, Eeyore. Drop in on any of us at any time, when you feel like it."

"Thank-you, Rabbit. And if anybody says in a Loud Voice 'Bother, it's Eeyore,' I can drop out again."

The House at Pooh Corner

"It's much better than mine," said Pooh admiringly, and he really thought it was.

"Well," explained Eeyore modestly, "it was meant to be."

The House at Pooh Corner

Rabbit sat down on the ground next to Pooh, and, feeling much less important like that, stood up again.

The House at Pooh Corner

If people ask me,
I always tell them:
"Quite well, thank you, I'm very
  glad to say."
If people ask me,
I always answer,
"Quite well, thank you, how are
  you to-day?"
I always answer,
I always tell them,
If they ask me
Politely . . .
BUT SOMETIMES

      I wish

           That they wouldn't.
      When We Were Very Young

"What about me?" said Pooh sadly. "I suppose *I* shan't be useful?"

"Never mind, Pooh," said Piglet comfortingly. "Another time perhaps."

Winnie-the-Pooh

"What I don't like about it is this," said Rabbit. "Here are we – you, Pooh, and you, Piglet, and Me – and suddenly—"

"And Eeyore," said Pooh.

"And Eeyore – and then suddenly—"

"And Owl," said Pooh.

"And Owl – and then all of a sudden—"

"Oh, and Eeyore," said Pooh. "I was forgetting *him*."

"Here – we – are," said Rabbit very slowly and carefully, "all – of – us, and then, suddenly, we wake up one morning, and what do we find? We find a Strange Animal among us. An animal of whom we had never even heard before! An animal who carries her family about with her in her pocket!"

Winnie-the-Pooh

118

"Thank you, Christopher Robin. You're the only one who seems to understand about tails. They don't think – that's what's the matter with some of these others. They've no imagination. A tail isn't a tail to *them*, it's just a Little Bit Extra at the back."

"Never mind, Eeyore," said Christopher Robin, rubbing his hardest. "Is *that* better?"

"It's feeling more like a tail perhaps. It Belongs again, if you know what I mean."

Winnie-the-Pooh

Rabbit came up importantly, nodded to Piglet, and said, "Ah, Eeyore," in the voice of one who would be saying "Good-bye" in about two more minutes.

The House at Pooh Corner

He was the sort of Tigger who was always in front when you were showing him the way anywhere, and was generally out of sight when at last you came to the place and said proudly "Here we are!"

The House at Pooh Corner

"*Well!*" said Kanga, and Roo fell in quickly, crying, "I *must* see Owl's sponge! Oh, there it is! Oh, Owl! Owl, it isn't a sponge, it's a spudge! Do you know what a spudge is, Owl? It's when your sponge gets all—" and Kanga said, "Roo, dear!" very quickly, because that's *not* the way to talk to anybody who can spell TUESDAY.

The House at Pooh Corner

Piglet had got up early that morning to pick himself a bunch of violets; and when he had picked them and put them in a pot in the middle of his house, it suddenly came over him that nobody had ever picked Eeyore a bunch of violets, and the more he thought of this, the more he thought how sad it was to be an Animal who had never had a bunch of violets picked for him. So he hurried out again, saying to himself, "Eeyore, Violets" and then "Violets, Eeyore," in case he forgot, because it was that sort of day.

The House at Pooh Corner

"I don't think you're helping," he said.

"No," said Pooh. "I do try," he added humbly.

Rabbit thanked him for trying.

The House at Pooh Corner

"Friends," he said, "including oddments, it is a great pleasure, or perhaps I had better say it has been a pleasure so far, to see you at my party. What I did was nothing. Any of you – except Rabbit and Owl and Kanga – would have done the same. Oh, and Pooh. My remarks do not, of course, apply to Piglet and Roo, because they are too small. Any of you would have done the same. But it just happened to be Me. It was not, I need hardly say, with an idea of getting what Christopher Robin is looking for now" – and he put his front leg to his mouth and said in a loud whisper, "Try under the table" – "that I did what I did – but because I feel that we should all do what we can to help."

Winnie-the-Pooh

"H – hup!" said Roo again.

"AS – I – WAS – SAYING," said Eeyore loudly and sternly, "as I was saying when I was interrupted by various Loud Sounds."

Winnie-the-Pooh

"Pooh!" he cried. "There's something climbing up your back."

"I thought there was," said Pooh.

"It's Small!" cried Piglet.

"Oh, *that's* who it is, is it?" said Pooh.

The House at Pooh Corner

"Hallo, Eeyore!" said Pooh. "This is Tigger."

"What is?" said Eeyore.

"This," explained Pooh and Piglet together, and Tigger smiled his happiest smile and said nothing.

Eeyore walked all round Tigger one way, and then turned and walked all round him the other way.

"What did you say it was?" he asked.

"Tigger."

"Ah!" said Eeyore.

"He's just come," explained Piglet.

"Ah!" said Eeyore again.

He thought for a long time and then said: "When is he going?"

The House at Pooh Corner

"It's Pooh," said Christopher Robin excitedly . . .

"Possibly," said Eeyore.

"*And* Piglet!" said Christopher Robin excitedly.

"Probably," said Eeyore. "What we *want* is a Trained Bloodhound."

The House at Pooh Corner

"I suppose none of you are sitting on a thistle by any chance?"

"I believe I am," said Pooh. "Ow!" He got up, and looked behind him. "Yes, I was. I thought so."

"Thank you, Pooh. If you've quite finished with it." He moved across to Pooh's place, and began to eat.

"It doesn't do them any Good, you know, sitting on them," he went on, as he looked up munching. "Takes all the Life out of them. Remember that another time, all of you. A little Consideration, a little Thought for Others, makes all the difference."

Winnie-the-Pooh

What shall we do about poor little
  Tigger?
If he never eats nothing he'll never
  get bigger.
He doesn't like honey and haycorns
  and thistles
Because of the taste and because
  of the bristles.
And all the good things which an
  animal likes
Have the wrong sort of swallow or
  too many spikes.

"He's quite big enough anyhow," said Piglet.

"He isn't *really* very big."

"Well, he *seems* so."

The House at Pooh Corner

"Everybody crowds round so in this Forest. There's no Space. I never saw a more Spreading lot of animals in my life, and all in the wrong places.

The House at Pooh Corner

Pooh said, "Let's go and see Kanga and Roo and Tigger," and Piglet said, "Y-yes. L-lets" – because he was still a little anxious about Tigger, who was a very Bouncy Animal, with a way of saying How-do-you-do, which always left your ears full of sand, even after Kanga had said, "Gently, Tigger dear," and had helped you up again.

The House at Pooh Corner

121

"That's what I call bouncing," said Eeyore. "Taking people by surprise. Very unpleasant habit. I don't mind Tigger being in the Forest," he went on, "because it's a large Forest, and there's plenty of room to bounce in it. But I don't see why he should come into *my* little corner of it, and bounce there. It isn't as if there was anything very wonderful about my little corner. Of course for people who like cold, wet, ugly bits it *is* something rather special, but otherwise it's just a corner, and if anybody feels bouncy—"

"I didn't bounce, I coughed," said Tigger crossly.

"Bouncy or coffy, it's all the same at the bottom of the river."

The House at Pooh Corner

122

Tigger was tearing round the Forest making loud yapping noises for Rabbit. And at last a very Small and Sorry Rabbit heard him. And the Small and Sorry Rabbit rushed through the mist at the noise, and it suddenly turned into Tigger; a Friendly Tigger, a Grand Tigger, a Large and Helpful Tigger, a Tigger who bounced, if he bounced at all, in just the beautiful way a Tigger ought to bounce.

"Oh, Tigger, I *am* glad to see you," cried Rabbit.

The House at Pooh Corner

"I should hate him to go *on* being Sad," said Piglet doubtfully.

"Tiggers never go on being Sad," explained Rabbit. "They get over it with Astonishing Rapidity. I asked Owl, just to make sure, and he said that that's what they always get over it with. But if we can make Tigger feel Small and Sad just for five minutes, we shall have done a good deed."

The House at Pooh Corner

Christopher Robin and Pooh and Piglet were left on the bridge by themselves.

For a long time they looked at the river beneath them, saying nothing, and the river said nothing too, for it felt very quiet and peaceful on this summer afternoon.

"Tigger is all right, *really*," said Piglet lazily.

"Of course he is," said Christopher Robin.

"Everybody is *really*," said Pooh. "That's what *I* think," said Pooh. "But I don't suppose I'm right," he said.

"Of course you are," said Christopher Robin.

The House at Pooh Corner

123

THAT SORT
OF BEAR

In which we find Quotations Just About Pooh

Sometimes Winnie-the-Pooh likes a game of some sort when he comes downstairs, and sometimes he likes to sit quietly in front of the fire and listen to a story. This evening—

"What about a story?" said Christopher Robin.

"*What* about a story?" I said.

"Could you very sweetly tell Winnie-the-Pooh one?"

"I suppose I could," I said. "What sort of stories does he like?"

"About himself. Because he's *that* sort of Bear."

"Oh, I see."

"So could you very sweetly?"

"I'll try," I said.

So I tried.

Winnie-the-Pooh

"Without Pooh," said Rabbit solemnly as he sharpened his pencil, "the adventure would be impossible."

"Oh!" said Piglet, and tried not to look to disappointed. But Pooh went into a corner of the room and said proudly to himself, "Impossible without Me! *That* sort of Bear."

Winnie-the-Pooh

Christopher Robin read the message aloud.

"Oh are those 'P's' piglets? I thought they were poohs."

The House at Pooh Corner

"Here it is!" cried Christopher Robin excitedly. "Pass it down to silly old Pooh. It's for Pooh."

"For Pooh?" said Eeyore.

"Of course it is. The best bear in all the world."

Winnie-the-Pooh

And then this Bear, Pooh Bear, Winnie-the-Pooh, F. O. P. (Friend of Piglet's), R. C. (Rabbit's Companion), P. D. (Pole Discoverer), E. C. and T. F. (Eeyore's Comforter and Tail-finder) – in fact, Pooh himself – said something so clever that Christopher Robin could only look at him with mouth open and eyes staring, wondering if this was really the Bear of Very Little Brain whom he had known and loved so long.

Winnie-the-Pooh

"A party for Me?" thought Pooh to himself. "How grand!"

Winnie-the-Pooh

"Oh, Bear!" said Christopher Robin. "How I do love you!"

"So do I," said Pooh.

Winnie-the-Pooh

INDEX